Praise for *For the Love*

A note from Jen Hatmaker

Before I wrote one word of this, I told all my Book People that I didn't want "celebrity endorsements." I wanted feedback from the same people I wrote it for: my real readers, my tribe. I put *For the Love* in the hands of my actual people, because it is their opinions I care about deeply. You can trust these girls, because they are us. Their loving words here are more than I can handle, so I'll just leave you with them before I come undone again.

"*For the Love* is like doing research on myself and discovering that I'm more okay than I thought. As someone in a similar stage of life as Jen, full of teenagers and undefined ailments, *For the Love* is like taking a deep breath."

—Anne Watson, speaker and author at GodDots.com

"If Jimmy Fallon and Ann Voskamp birthed a literary love child they'd have to name it *For the Love*."

—Danielle Brower, wife, mom, lover of love, orphan advocate

"If you've ever been broken—if you've ever been hurting and needed a safe place to come home to, this is the book for you. Let Jen and Jesus wrap their arms around you and grace begin to do its healing work."

—Stacey Philpot, wife, mom, minister of the Gospel, aspiring author

"Jen put words to realities that my heart has been feeling but couldn't fully express. This book made me laugh as much as it made me cry, stirred my soul, and left me feeling like Jen was patting me on the back, encouraging me to step into all that God has for me in this one life that I get."

—Katie Tramonte, introvert, blogger,
Jesus-follower, lover of free swag

"If you're looking for just another Christian book by just another Christian author, this is not the book for you. Jen transcends the lines between Christian and secular culture through her humor and personable nature. Identifying the common threads that run through each of us, regardless of faith, creates a platform for women to be united. *For the Love* is the book you place into the hands of every woman in your life, believer or unbeliever."

—Katie Howard, boy mom, pastor's wife, closet blogger

"I want to carry a basket full of copies of this book with me everywhere I go and hand them out to every woman I see."

—Traci Cook, Christ follower, Army wife, mom of 2 boys, Baylor
girl, educator, sometimes-blogger, social media enthusiast

"I've read this book three times in two months. Jen's words are like a breath of fresh air that encourage me to take off some pressure, put on a whole lot of love, and believe that it will be enough."

—Gina Grizzle, wife, mom, blogger, lover of
words and ice cream in waffle cones

"*For the Love* is stellar. You will not find another bunch of words put together that make you want to love God, love others, and fight for scandalous grace like this book does."

—Tomi Cheeks, wife to my hero; mother to a child in college,
kindergarten, and preschool; freed-up daughter of the King;
professional people watcher; lover of junk, Texas, stretchy pants,
big hair, gathering my peeps, feathering my nest, books, and glitter

"In the midst of my uncontrollable laughter I saw the ever-present grace and mercy and hope of Jesus shining through. This is a book for the 'every woman!' "

—Krista Wilbur, blogger, Netflix aficionado, dog lover

"Jen pulls you close and whispers in your ear, 'You are not failing. You're doing great!' And because of Jen's authenticity and her gift with words and with people, you actually believe her, breathe a sigh of relief, and feel empowered to go out and be a little gentler with everybody else, too."

—Jennifer Wier, writer, counselor, community-builder

"From start to finish, this book makes you feel like you are having coffee with your best friend. It's fun, encouraging, thought provoking, and leaves you with a renewed love for life, people, and Jesus."

—Elise Johnson, wife, mom, blogger, caffeine addict

"Don't be surprised if you get to the end and want to immediately start all over again!"

—April Lakata Cao, military wife, mom to
four extraordinary kids, and writer

"*For the Love* is a breath of fresh air, a relevant call to action, and an invitation for women to let ourselves 'off the hook' so that we can get real about living and loving freely and boldly."

—Amanda Johnson, harmonica collector, embracer and
contributor of awkward situations, guacamole lover

"This book will have you crying, dying of laugher (seriously to tears), and saying, 'Hallelujah! I am not the only one that feels that way!' This is a book not to pass up sistas! Bust a move and get it!"

—Jennie Woelpern, book addict, blogger (@ajourney4life)

"If I would have read this book when I was a 'young one' I'm certain my life would have been richer and fuller and I would have experienced so much more freedom."

—Andrea Stunz, homemaker, foodie, and pilgrim in need of grace and coffee

"Read this book, but not in public . . . unless you are okay with being the only one laughing out loud in a silent room or ugly crying at chapter 11 while other people pretend not to stare. If you are okay with those things, then you should totally read this book in public. Otherwise, I recommend good coffee, comfy jammies, and a locked door."

—Emily Donehoo, writer, speaker, actual human

"*For the Love* is a must read book. You'll laugh, cry, shout in agreement, and want to read all of it aloud to your unsuspecting children, house guests, friends and/or husband."

—Alyssa DeLosSantos, wife of John, mother of three lovelies, ragamuffin, accidental blogger

"Jen nailed it! Everything. Nailed. Couldn't put the book down, I was hooked. And, when I finally finished it, I picked it back up and started reading again!"

—Brandy Lidbeck, marriage and family therapist, humor enthusiast

"Jen Hatmaker writes in such a conversational way, it's more like having coffee and great conversation with friends than reading a book (no wonder everyone thinks she should be their new best friend!)."

—Cindy Battles, mother, Jesus follower, coffee addict

"*For the Love* will be a well-loved, often reread favorite on my bookshelf for years to come and will be my perfect 'go-to' gift for all occasions . . . because who doesn't need a healthy dose of laughter and grace and Jen Hatmaker on a regular basis?"

—Julie Shreve, real estate broker, blogger, everyone's favorite aunt

"Whether lamenting the tragedy of 'tights as leggings,' rejoicing in the blessing of good food or challenging her readers to live with big hearts, Jen Hatmaker cuts to the soul of what it means to be a woman."

—Marie Gregg, blogger, librarian, eater of chocolate

"This book is like spending a weekend with Jen in which you discuss all the things using all the words and feeling all the feels. You'll laugh, cry, think, and be challenged to be the best you."

—Ann Goade, wife, mom, and still figuring out what to be when I grow up

"Jen does an outstandingly witty job of exposing the truth to the untouched places of motherhood, friendships, fashion, life, and so much more."

—Amanda Brown, wife, mother, teacher, and artist

"Y'all . . . do not open this book unless you are ready to be wrecked by the gospel."

—Hannah Card, wanderer and wonderer, passionate pursuer of Jesus, coffee

"*For the Love* is a breath of fresh air in a world where one's Christian beliefs can often be a dividing rather than uniting force."

—Sandy Kaduce, freelance writer, blogger, and mom

For the Love

FIGHTING *for* GRACE
in a World of Impossible Standards

Jen Hatmaker

NELSON
BOOKS

An Imprint of Thomas Nelson

Published in Nashville, Tennessee, by Nelson Books, an imprint of Thomas Nelson. Nelson Books and Thomas Nelson are registered trademarks of HarperCollins Christian Publishing, Inc.

Published in association with Yates & Yates, www.yates2.com.

Thomas Nelson titles may be purchased in bulk for educational, business, fundraising, or sales promotional use. For information, please e-mail SpecialMarkets@ThomasNelson.com.

Library of Congress Control Number: 2015931078

ISBN: 978-0-7180-3182-4 (HC)
ISBN: 978-0-7180-3784-0 (IE)

Printed in the United States of America

15 16 17 18 19 RRD 6 5

For Jesus, who taught me how to love people.

Contents

Introduction   xiii

Your Very Own Self

1. Worst Beam Ever   3

2. On Turning Forty   10

3. On Calling and Haitian Moms   17

4. Fashion Concerns   24

5. Run Your Race   30

6. Not Buying   35

7. Tell the Truth   43

8. Thank-You Notes (Part 1)   50

All These People Who Live in Your House

9. Hope for Spicy Families   57

10. Surviving School   63

11. Dear Kids   70

12. Marriage: Have Fun and Stuff   77

13. Jesus Kids   86

14. Thank-You Notes (Part 2)   96

Friends, Neighbors, Strangers, and Enemies

15. Supper Club   103

16. Porches as Altars   113

17. Quirky   120

18. Difficult People   130

19. Bonus Supper Club Menu   140

20. Thank-You Notes (Part 3)   147

Church, Church People, Not-Church People, and God

21. Poverty Tourism   153

22. Dear Church . . .   161

23. If Social Media Were Around   175

24. Thank-You Notes (Part 4)   185

25. Dear Christians, Please Stop Being Lame   189

26. On Women   198

Conclusion   205

Thank-You Notes For Real (Acknowledgments)   209

Notes   217

About the Author   221

Introduction

My girlfriend relayed a story to me recently about her conversation with my youngest daughter, Remy:

> GF: Tell me about your mom's job, Remy.
> REMY: Oh, she doesn't really have one.
> GF: I'm pretty sure your mom works.
> REMY: Yeah, but she doesn't have a job where she *knows* about something.
> GF: So she just writes books about nothing?
> REMY: Well, she also cooks a lot.

Besides being obviously esteemed in my own home, maybe I ought to clarify what exactly I specialize in, since it appears very, very unclear to my own child. Certain folks love numbers and columns and reconciled accounts. (I barely even know what this means.) Some of my good friends love organizing and administrating; they are weirdly good at it. I have family members who excel at web design and creative technology and others who are craftsmen and builders. Educators, chefs, sports medicine specialists, realtors: all people in my circle who obviously *know about something*.

A little closer to my space, some of my girlfriends are true theologians and love the ins and outs of sticky hermeneutics. Others are preachers with fire in their bellies. Some are academics working on graduate degrees in God. Some are social entrepreneurs doing great good with their companies and organizations. Still others give their lives to justice in hard places. This is how they are gifted and this is what they love.

I love people.

It's what I know.

God has always made the most sense to me through people, His image bearers. I crave dignity and healing and purpose and freedom for me and mine, you and yours, them and theirs. I want us to live well and love well. The substance of life isn't stuff or success or work or accomplishments or possessions. It really isn't, although we devote enormous energy to those goals. The fullest parts of my life, the best memories, the most satisfying pieces of my story have always involved people. Conversely, nothing hurts worse or steals more joy than broken relationships. We can heal and hurt each other, and we do.

I'm hoping to help lead a tribe that does more healing and less hurting.

I consider that my job.

I see a generation of people ON THE HOOK. Man, we are

tough on one another, starting with ourselves. When Jesus said to "love your neighbor as yourself," I don't think He meant judgmentally; but that is exactly how we treat our own souls, so it bleeds out to others. Folks who thrive in God's grace give grace easily, but the self-critical person becomes others-critical. We "love" people the way we "love" ourselves, and if we are not good enough, then no one is.

We keep ourselves brutally on the hook, plus our husbands, our kids, our friends, our churches, our leaders, anyone "other." When we impose unrealistic expectations on ourselves, it's natural to force them on everyone else. If we're going to fail, at least we can expect others to fail; and misery loves company, right?

I believe we can do better than this. I think God wants us off the hook, since Jesus pretty much already handled that for us. Can I tell you my dream for this little book? I hope you close the last page and breathe an enormous sigh of relief. I hope you laugh out loud because you just got *free*. Then I hope you look with fresh, renewed eyes at all your people—that one you married, those ones you birthed, the ones on your street and in your church and at your work and around the world—and you are released to love them as though it is your job.

Maybe we can lay down our fear and criticism, self-directed and otherwise. Maybe if we let ourselves off the hook, we can let others off, too, and discover that God was in control all along, just as He tried to tell us. He is good at being God. Hooray! We don't have to be saviors and critics for each other; we're probably better as loved people beside one another.

We aren't good gods, but we can be good humans.

Spoiler alert: You are amazing. You are. This grace thing is no joke. We get to live a free life. So do other people because God gave us Jesus, who fixed everything. Instead of being "right" at each other all the time, we can just live these beautiful, precious lives of ours in full freedom. It really is good news.

I have an oft-quoted pet phrase I abuse with regularity: *for the love.* (Its cousins include "for crying out loud" and "good grief" and "for Pete's sake" because dramatic hyperbole is my medium.) I use it all the time in ways that make sense and in ways that utterly don't. I find it a delightful catchall response:

For the love of Moses.

For the love of Tina Turner.

For the love of Coach and Tami Taylor.

There is really no end to its uses. As this book started taking shape and I discovered its contents, the title became instantly clear: *For the Love.*

This is why we live and breathe: for the love of Jesus, for the love of our own souls, for the love of our families and people, for the love of our neighbors and this world. This is all that will last. Honestly, it is all that matters. Because as Paul basically said: We can have our junk together in a thousand areas, but if we don't have love, we are totally bankrupt. Get this right and everything else follows. Get it wrong, and life becomes bitter, fear-based, and lonely. Dear ones, it doesn't have to be.

Love is really the most excellent way.

One of the best parts of being human is other humans. It's true, because life is hard; but people get to show up for one another, as God told us to, and we remember we are loved and seen and God is here and we are not alone. We can't deliver folks from their pits, but we can sure get in there with them until God does. Live long enough and it becomes clear that stuff is not the stuff of life. People are. We need each other, so we probably ought to practice radical grace, because our well-flaunted opinions are cold companions when real life hits.

So grab my hand, good reader. I'll tell you how amazing you are, how shockingly gracious God is, and how free we are to love well. I hope to lift every noose from your neck, both the ones you put there and the ones someone else did. We are going to let ourselves and each other off the hook, and in the end, we will be free to run our races well; to live wide, generous days; and to practice the wholehearted living we were created for.

Oh! I will also be discussing high-waisted jeans and Netflix addictions, so you have a lot of substance ahead of you.

This is going to be so fun.

YOUR VERY
OWN SELF

CHAPTER I

Worst Beam Ever

My nine-year-old daughter Remy is in gymnastics. After her second practice, she asked when she would have her first competition. Bless. No one ever accused that one of low self-esteem. (She is currently deciding between a future as a professional gymnast or a singer, and may I just say that both plan A and plan B are fatally flawed?)

She struggles most with the balance beam. It's unclear who invented this particular apparatus, but it was certainly not the mother of a gangly third-grader with delusions of grandeur. She is still attempting to get from one end to the other with a few "dips" and "scoops" and "leans" without falling to the mat. Forget the fancy moves; just one notch above walking throws her so off-kilter, I am beginning to wonder how she will ever become an Olympian with a music career on the side.

If I had to recite the top questions I'm asked in interviews, conversations, and e-mails, certainly included would be this one:

3

How do you balance work and family and community?

And every time, I think: *Do you even know me?*

Balance. It's like a unicorn; we've heard about it, everyone talks about it and makes airbrushed T-shirts celebrating it, it seems super rad, but we haven't actually seen one. I'm beginning to think it isn't a thing.

Here is part of the problem, girls: we've been sold a bill of goods. Back in the day, women didn't run themselves ragged trying to achieve some impressively developed life in eight different categories. No one constructed fairy-tale childhoods for their spawn, developed an innate set of personal talents, fostered a stimulating and world-changing career, created stunning homes and yardscapes, provided homemade food for every meal (locally sourced, of course), kept all marriage fires burning, sustained meaningful relationships in various environments, carved out plenty of time for "self care," served neighbors/church/world, and maintained a fulfilling, active relationship with Jesus our Lord and Savior.

You can't balance that job description.

Listen to me: No one can pull this off. No one *is* pulling this off. The women who seem to ride this unicorn only display the best parts of their stories. Trust me. No one can fragment her time and attention into this many segments.

The trouble is, we have up-close access to women who excel in each individual sphere. With social media and its carefully selected messaging, we see career women killing it, craft moms slaying it, chef moms nailing it, Christian leaders working it. We register their beautiful yards, homemade green chile enchiladas, themed birthday parties, eight-week Bible study series, chore charts, ab routines,

"10 Tips for a Happy Marriage," career best practices, volunteer work, and Family Fun Night ideas. We make note of their achievements, cataloging their successes and observing their talents. Then we combine the best of everything we see, every woman we admire in every genre, and conclude: *I should be all of that.*

It is certifiably insane.

The only thing worse than this unattainable standard is the guilt that follows when perfection proves impossible. Sister, what could be crazier than a woman who wakes children up before dawn, feeds and waters them while listening and affirming all their chatter, gets them dressed and off to school with signed folders, then perhaps heads to a job to put food on the table or stays home to raise littles who cannot even wipe, completes one million domestic chores that multiply like gremlins, breaks up forty-four fights, intentionally disciplines 293 times a day, attends to all e-mails/correspondence/deadlines, helps with math/writing/biology homework, serves dinner while engineering a round of "High-Low," oversees Bedtime and Bath Marathon, reads lovingly to lap children, tucks them in with prayers, finishes the endless Daily Junk Everywhere Pickup, turns attention to husband with either mind or body, then has one last thought of the day: *I am doing a terrible job at everything.*

I feel like I'm taking crazy pills.

This is beyond unreasonable. It is destructive. We no longer assess our lives with any accuracy. We have lost the ability to declare a job well-done. We measure our performance against an *invented standard* and come up wanting, and it is destroying our joy. No matter how hard we work or excel in an area or two, it never feels like enough. Our primary defaults are exhaustion and guilt.

Meanwhile, we have beautiful lives begging to be really lived, really enjoyed, really applauded—and it is simpler than we dare hope: we gotta unload that beam.

We cannot do it all, have it all, or master it all. That is simply not a thing. May I tell you something? Because women ask constantly how I "do it all," let me clear something up: I HAVE HELP. My booking representative handles events, my literary agent manages publishing stuff, my tech person does all the Internet things, my extraordinary housekeepers do in two hours what would take me twelve, and our part-time nanny fills in the gaps.

I'm not doing it all. Who could? I can't. You can't. I decided what tricks belonged on my beam and dropped the rest or figured out a way to delegate. I love to write but hate web management. Off the beam. I could not juggle weekend travel, weeknight activities (times five kids . . . be near, Jesus), and a weekly small group, so as much as I love our church people, we aren't in a group right now. (And I am the pastor's wife, so let that speak freedom over your *shoulds*.) Off the beam.

Cooking and sit-down dinners? Life-giving for me. On the beam.

Coffee with everyone who wants to "pick my brain"? I simply can't. Off the beam.

After-hours with our best friends on the patio? Must. On the beam.

Classroom Mom? I don't have the skill set. Off the beam.

You get to do this too. You have permission to examine all

the tricks and decide what should stay. What parts do you love? What are you good at? What brings you life? What *has* to stay during this season? *Don't look sideways for these answers.* Don't transplant someone else's keepers onto your beam. I could cook for days, but this does not mean you want to. Classroom Mom for me would mean a nervous breakdown; it might be the high-light of your year. You do you here. There are only twenty-four hours in a day.

We need to quit trying to be awesome and instead be wise.

Decide which parts are draining you dry. What do you dread? What are you including for all the wrong reasons? Which parts are for approval? Is there anything you could delegate or hand off? Could you sacrifice a Good for a Best? Throw out every *should* or *should not* and make ruthless cuts. Go ahead. Your beam is too crowded. I know it.

Frame your choices through this lens: season. If your kids are under five, you cannot possibly include the things I can with middle and high schoolers. You are ruled by a tiny army you created yourself. This is just how it is right now. If you have bigs like I do, we run a taxi service from 5:00 to 9:00 p.m. virtually every night. Evening real estate belongs to family for now. In ten years when they are gone, the story will change (*sob*). Perhaps you have a fabulous trick that no longer works, and you might need to set it aside for a season. Those are often the hardest cuts. The choices you make today may completely change in five years or even next year. Operate in the right-now.

What does this season require of you? Unsure? Ask God. He is a wonderful advisor who always, always knows the Best Thing.

He will help you sort it out. When you can't trust your own discernment, you can certainly trust His. God has no agenda other than your highest good in His kingdom. There is no better leader through this minefield.

I labored over a scheduling decision last year, and the drama I projected was undoubtedly annoying. I fretted and agonized and vacillated before I remembered to pray. (I am a delightful choice for your spiritual advisor, yes?) I kid you not: I finally gave the decision to God, and in five seconds, it was instantly clear. The answer was no and it probably saved my life.

By the way, no one will make these choices for you. People will take as much as you will give them, not because they are terrible humans, but because they only want this one slice of you. It doesn't seem like much to them. On paper, it's just that one thing, that one night, that one commitment. Plus, you're probably good at their pet thing. But they don't observe the scope of your life and all the other tricks on your beam. They just want that one dip/scoop/lean, but only so many tricks fit into a day.

Good news: most people are surprisingly respectful with boundaries. Folks take a no better than I suspected. When I say, "Thank you for inviting me into this good thing of yours. It is as extraordinary as you are. But any new yes I give means a no to my family and sanity. Please accept my sincere regrets and count on my prayers," most people are amazing. You can say no, and no one will die. In fact, gracious noes challenge the myth of Doing It All. When I see another woman fighting for her balance beam, I am inspired because if she has permission, then I do too. Wise women know what to hold onto and what to release, and how to walk confidently in their choices—no regrets, no apologies, no guilt.

I deeply believe God wants this freedom for us. Scripture instructs us to live presently and joyfully, resisting worry and believing Jesus set us free for freedom's sake. We have an abundance of good and perfect gifts that often look like a messy house full of laughter, a ten-year-old running through a sprinkler, a heart unburdened by comparison, an afternoon nap, joy in using our gifts and leaving the rest to people better suited. Our generation is so hamstrung with striving and guilt, we no longer recognize God's good and perfect gifts staring us in the face. What a tragedy. What a loss. We will never get these lovely years back.

So no, you cannot balance an overloaded beam. That is not a possibility. But maybe if we reject the invented standard, if we stop fearing a no will end the world, if we pare our lives down to what is beautiful, essential, life-giving, if we refuse to guilt one another for different choices, and if we celebrate the decent accomplishments of Ordinary Good Hard Life, then we'll discover there wasn't a beam in the first place, that God's kingdom never required a balancing act, and Jesus was in that fun foam pit all along.

We are all Olympic hopefuls in *that* event.

CHAPTER 2

On Turning Forty

I am experiencing trauma and am unsure what to do. It blindsides me constantly, assaulting me when I am unaware and unprepared. Every time, I am left reeling and need to lie down to recover. I never get used to it, and each time it happens is like the first time.

I keep seeing someone's old-lady hands sticking out of my sleeves.

There I am, just going about my work, and BAM. Old-lady hands typing. Reaching for my dishes and KAPOW. Old-lady hands cooking. These hands are quite confusing, with their veins and sunspots and loose skin. What in the actual heck? Whose grandma hands are wearing my jewelry? More specifically, how did my mother's exact hands relocate to my body? My friend Tray went to high school with a woman who was convinced the government had transplanted different hands onto her body in some conspiracy (bless), and even as I chuckle, I'm secretly thinking, *It's all starting to make sense.*

I turned forty this year.

Forty! Which is so weird because I've always been young. I've been young my whole life, as a matter of fact. No matter how I dissect this, I've aged out of the "young" category and graduated to the "middle" group. My brain feels confused about this because I am so juvenile. I make up my own words to hip-hop songs and quote Paul Rudd as a parenting strategy. Surely I am a preteen. But much like Shakira: these hands don't lie.

So gather round, young things, for I know you think me ancient. You think forty is so distant it cannot be comprehended, though basic math confirms it a mere, say, eleven years away. In my twenties, I pitied the middle-aged as they clearly had one foot in the grave. *I will never be forty*, thought my young, deluded self. *I will always have this elastic body and newborn-baby hands. My forehead will appear kissed by angels every morning. I will pee only if and when I want to.*

Well, let me and my fellow fortysomethings tell you about it. We don't mean to terrify, but you need to know some truths. We don't want you wringing your hands in eleven years crying, "Nobody tooooooold me!" So grab a pen while I prepare you for some things.

Something weird happens to your brain. This brain has served you well for so long, but it starts punking you. You can't remember directions, you forget why you walked into a room, and for the life of you, you can't recall your third kid's name ("Take out the trash . . . I want to say . . . Chris?"). You will talk on your cell phone while looking around your house for your cell phone. No one helps because they are laughing at you; these people you live with mock this behavior. Sometimes your husband will say a sentence using English words, but for some reason, the sentence won't compute and you will stare at him blankly, like a pigeon, because the words are so confusing. *What is he trying to say? What are these words? Is this a trick? Talking is hard.*

And the learning. Heaven help if you need to learn something new. At this point, education is a fool's errand. Your brain is not helpful. It is done. It already took you to college and did the heavy lifting for the last twenty years, and now it is taking a cigarette break. This is unfortunate because about this time you go back to middle and high school with your spawn. You are expected to help with algebra and chemistry and the remembering of all the things, but your brain resembles the bottom of your purse: lost pen caps and congealed, undefined filth. It feels furious about the chemistry homework. It feels angry about this new math. It will not have this crap. It will take a nap while those children work their own stuff out. Your brain already completed eleventh grade. It has done its time.

We are sorry to disclose this, young ones, but you can no longer quit eating bread for one day and lose six pounds. I know this is hard to believe. I once thought that if I made minor adjustments and took a jog, those tight jeans would fit by Tuesday. Your body is over this by forty. It just wants to be fat and happy. To prove its point, you can eat four hundred calories a day for six weeks and your body will release three pounds. The next day you eat half a tortilla and gain seventeen. It isn't interested in your diet or those jeans. Your body wants yoga pants and your husband's stretched-out T-shirts, and it will have them. Enjoy your young body. Walk naked past full-length mirrors. Wear your bikini to the grocery store. Take a lot of pictures because when you see a photo of your twenty-nine-year-old self one day, you will weep at your smooth thighs.

Skin. Come close, all ye still bathing in the fountain of youth: TAKE CARE OF YOUR SKIN. I know, you'll never be old and wrinkly and being tan is *just the best*, but you'll soon regret this folly. It's strange with the skin, because sometimes your brain helps you survive the bathroom mirror (remember it is addled, plus denial is strong, young Jedi), but then you see a picture of yourself and you're like, *I was in some terrible lighting and also the angle is tragic plus the shadows made my neck look weird and for the love of Annie Leibovitz do my friends not know how to use INSTAGRAM FILTERS?* It is all very distressing. Sometimes I baby-talk parts of my body into resisting the mutiny: "Come on, Shins. I'm counting on you. You've always been good to me. You don't want to be like Neck and Eyelids and Chest, those loose floozies. Hang in there, baby, and you'll be the last part of me to see the light of day."

You will be surprised, but you'll become a crotchety grandma about certain things. Now you think, *Wooohoo, y'all! Burn down the establishment! We are young and beautiful and we embrace this big life with wide-open arms! Down with The Man! Go big or go home!* But in a few years you will sound more like, *Settle down, young man, some of us need to get some sleep.* My girlfriend went dancing with her husband last week, and it took her three days to recover. Brandon bought front-row balcony tickets to Aerosmith to ensure I could sit down. (I can't stand for three hours. I'm not an Olympian.) You will avoid crowds, bemoan today's youth, disparage the kids' music, and ninja-sneak out of parties to go home and watch *House Hunters*. This is your future. Make your peace.

You've always been pop culture savvy, but something strange happens around forty. I wonder at the cover of *US Weekly*: *Who are these people and why can't that girl exit a car without flashing her bits and nubs?* After one episode of *Keeping Up with the Kardashians*, you declare America intellectually bankrupt. (See former paragraph about crotchety grandma behavior.) Who are these teenaged singers? How do this many college-aged kids have TV shows? What are the popular baby names now? Is the name *Emma* so 2002? We have no idea. I don't know that song, that series, or that star. I still watch *Friends* reruns almost every night. Just whatever, man.

Now listen, sweet young thing. In case you've lost the will to live, there is some good news too. You won't *just* be a wrinkled, cranky chub who can't find her glasses while wearing them. You get some other goodies besides incontinence.

You get a decent handle on who you are, what you are good at, what you love, what you value, and how you want to live. These questions used to keep me up at night. Young one, if you worry endlessly about purpose and trajectory, identity and worth, forty brings security you can't imagine. I know what I am good at now and I do it. I'm not apologetic and uncertain and aw-shucks about running my race. I no longer tiptoe through my own life, doubting my gifts and my place, too scared to go for it, seize it, pray for it, dream it. When you're forty, you no longer wait for permission to live. It's time, and as Maya Angelou said, "Life loves the liver of it."[1]

In the same way, I don't look sideways as much. Oh my stars, when I was twenty-nine, I was so hamstrung by what everyone else was accomplishing. Other people were my benchmarks, and comparison stole entire years. I lost much time in jealousy, judgment, and imitation. I just couldn't find my own song. I struggled to celebrate others' achievements because they felt like indictments on my uncertainty. Now fully able to cheer wildly for friends and colleagues, I am free to be me without the constrictive mesh netting around my heart, everyone else is free to be themselves, and I am thrilled about us all.

By forty you develop resiliency. I needed approval desperately even ten years ago. Criticism crushed me. Conflict paralyzed me. Disapproval evaporated me. Consequently, I took the safest path through every scenario to avoid reproach. As a former approval addict, I would have been shocked to find that to some degree, your forty-year-old self won't care much what anyone thinks of you, your parenting, your marriage, your career, your politics, your house, your wardrobe, your hair, your kids, your choices, your church, your dog, your new red front door, your comfortable flats, your stretchy pants, your daughter's hair, your son's weird interest in vintage ska, your favorite college sweatshirt you still wear, your decision to homeschool/private school/public school, your new resolve to go vegan, your consistent purchase of Lunchables, your decision to work, your decision to quit, your random idea to purchase chickens. It just won't matter. If people don't like it, well, tra la la. It's not that you become unteachable or unleadable or uncorrectable; differing opinions just stop shaking every decision, and critical words won't send you to bed. You develop chops, sister. You're going to love it.

You settle in. These kids, this husband, this little life you're building . . . you say *amen*. You are slower to tell everyone how wrong they are and quicker to gather your folks and breathe gratitude. This is your place. These are your people. This is your beautiful, precious life. Probably about halfway done here on earth, you lay down angst and pick up contentment.

Annie Dillard was right: "How we spend our days is, of course, how we spend our lives."[2] You decide your days should contain laughter and grace, strength and security. You real-ize insecurity, striving, jealousy, and living in comparison will eventually define your entire life, and that is not the legacy you want. Let the young whippersnappers duke it out; you and your people are busy enjoying a bottle of wine on the deck.

So sure, your body and mind get whack, but I promise: you wouldn't return to your twenties for all the unwrinkled skin on earth. You'll like it here. You will love better, stand taller, laugh louder. You'll pass out grace like candy. Real life will temper your arrogance and fear, and you will adore the next version of yourself. We all will.

But just in case, wear sunscreen every day, for the love.

CHAPTER 3

On Calling and Haitian Moms

Don't ever confuse the two, your life and your work.
That's what I have to say.
The second is only a part of the first. . . .
There are thousands of people out there with the same
degree you have; when you get a job, there will be
thousands of people doing what you want to do for a
living.
But you are the only person alive who has sole custody of
your life.
Your particular life. Your entire life.
Not just your life at a desk, or your life on the bus, or in
the car, or at the computer.
Not just the life of your mind, but the life of your heart.

—ANNA QUINDLEN[1]

It has taken me forty years to assess the difference between the gospel and the American evangelical version of the gospel. Those were one and the same for ages—no take-backs, no prisoners, no holds barred. I filtered the kingdom through my upper middle-class, white, advantaged, denominational lens, and by golly, I found a way to make most of it fit! (It was a complicated task, but I managed. Please be impressed.)

But then God changed my life, and everything got weird. I discovered the rest of the world! And other cultures! And different Christian traditions! And people who were way, way different from me! And poverty! Then the system in which God operated according to my rules started disintegrating. I started hearing my gospel narrative through the ears of the Other, and a giant whole bunch of it didn't even make sense. Some values and perspectives and promises I attributed to God's own heart only worked in my context, and I'm no theologian, but surely that is problematic.

There is a biblical benchmark I now use. We will refer to this criterion for every hard question, big idea, topic, assessment of our own obedience, every "should" or "should not" and "will" or "will not" we ascribe to God, every theological sound bite. Here it is: *If it isn't also true for a poor single Christian mom in Haiti, it isn't true.*

If a sermon promises health and wealth to the faithful, it isn't true, because that theology makes God an absolute monster who only blesses rich westerners and despises Christians in Africa, India, China, South America, Russia, rural Appalachia, inner-city America, and everywhere else a sincere believer remains poor. If it isn't also true for a poor single Christian mom in Haiti, it isn't true.

If doctrine elevates a woman's married-with-children status as her highest calling, it isn't true, because that omits single believers (whose status Paul considered preferable), widows, the childless by choice or fate or loss, the divorced, and the celibate gay. If these folks are second-class citizens in the kingdom because they aren't married with children, then God just excluded millions of people from gospel work, and I guess they should just eat rocks and die. If it isn't also true for a poor single Christian mom in Haiti, it isn't true.

Theology is either true everywhere or it isn't true anywhere. This helps untangle us from the American God Narrative and sets God free to be God instead of the My-God-in-a-Pocket I carried for so long. It lends restraint when declaring what God does or does not think, because sometimes my portrayal of God's ways sounds suspiciously like the American Dream and I had better check myself. Because of the Haitian single mom. Maybe I should speak less for God.

This brings me to the question at hand, another popular subject I am asked to pontificate on: *What is my calling?* (See also: *How do I know my calling? When did you know your calling? How can I get your calling? Has God told you my calling? Can you get me out of my calling?*)

Ah yes, "The Calling." This is certainly a favorite Christian concept over in these parts. Here is the trouble: Scripture barely confirms our elusive calling—the bull's-eye, life purpose, individual mission every hardworking Protestant wants to discover.

I found five scriptures, three of which referred to salvation rather than a job description (Rom. 11:29, 2 Peter 1:10, and Heb. 3:1). Here are the other two:

"As a prisoner for the Lord, then, I urge you to live a life worthy of the calling you have received" (Eph. 4:1).

"With this in mind, we constantly pray for you, that our God may make you worthy of his calling, and that by his power he may bring to fruition your every desire for goodness and your every deed prompted by faith" (2 Thess. 1:11).

Contextually, God's calling here is broad, mainly referring to that great, glorious mystery where God makes us family. The call is the invitation; the worthy life and "desire for goodness" and "every deed prompted by faith" are the fully unspecified results. This framework holds true for any believer anywhere. Worthy lives bloom under the nourishment of grace in every context, every country. Goodness, desired and implemented, is demonstrated by Christians wherever they've been set free.

Good reader, I don't mean to vilify your search for a calling, because I share the desire for purpose. Rather, I want to loosen some of its manufactured chains. I see women pressing pause on their present lives while waiting to decode their "callings." *When my kids are bigger, then I'll . . . When my platform is larger, then I'll . . . When I'm better at what I do, then I'll . . . When I get a lightning bolt from heaven, then I'll . . .*

In many ways, the perception of calling is a luxury of the privileged. A life's purpose need not be authenticated by a business plan, a 501c3, a website, a salary, or an audience. We get to labor over our "calling" because we are educated and financially stable, so many of us eschew the honor of ordinary work and instead fret over the perception of wasting our lives.

Our single mom in Haiti entertains none of this. She works hard because she has to. She isn't attempting to discern an elusive calling. She is raising her babies, working for a living, doing the best she can with what she has. Her purpose may not venture outside the walls of her home. We will never know her name. She probably won't step into leadership or innovation or advocacy or social revolution.

Yet she is also worthy of the calling she has received.

A worthy life involves loving as loved folks do, sharing the ridiculous mercy God spoiled us with first. (It really is ridiculous.) It means restoring people, in ordinary conversations and regular encounters. A worthy life means showing up when showing up is the only thing to do. Goodness bears itself out in millions of ordinary ways across the globe, for the rich and poor, the famous and unknown, in enormous measures and tiny, holy moments. It may involve a career and it may not. It may include traditional components and it may not.

To Mama at home with a bunch of littles, you can live a life worthy right now. Your calling is today. God makes you worthy as you desire goodness for your children, meeting needs and nurturing little souls. No future calling is any more important than your current station. Every good, meaningful possibility is yours today. You have access to the kingdom now: the love, joy, peace, patience, kindness, goodness, faithfulness, gentleness, and self-control. That is every Christian's calling, and the gospel is perfectly demonstrated through the daily labor of parenting.

Hard worker, punching the clock and paying the bills, you can live a life worthy this day. Your career may not involve "Christian-sanctioned" labor, but that doesn't mean you aren't walking in your calling. The manner in which you speak to your coworkers, the way you work diligently, your dignity as a laborer worth her wages—this is a worthy life. Every goodness God asked us to display is available to you today. Through ordinary work, people can be set free, valued, and changed, including yourself. God's kingdom will not come in any more power elsewhere than it will come in your life today.

Visionary, super tapped into what feels like your life's work, you're wonderful. Some make a career out of what they love. But your calling doesn't begin and end with your job. The gutters are lined with folks who are burned-out from the frenzy of their work. Calling is a big umbrella under which "career" lives. It is one piece of your assignment, but if it fizzles or bombs or shifts or disappears, you can still live a worthy life full of faith-prompted deeds and goodness.

Maybe we can exit the self-imposed pressure cooker of "calling" and instead just consider our "gifts." The former feels like a job description, but the latter is just how God wired us. Certainly we are gifted for specific faith work, but gifts can be ordinary stuff in the middle of real life. Your prayer gift? You can use it on random Thursdays, on the phone with a friend, in the quiet of early morning hours. Your gift of teaching? It may look like a class or career, but it could very well be over lunch, through an e-mail, or in your own home. Your special capacity for encouragement? Sister, that gift is needed everywhere, every day, for every person.

This is your calling.

This makes perfect sense to our single mom in Haiti.

You don't need to wait another day to figure out your calling. You're living it, dear one. Your gifts have a place right now, in the job you have, in your stage of life, with the people who surround you. Calling is virtually never big or famous work; that is rarely the way the kingdom comes. It shows up quietly, subversively, almost invisibly. Half the time, it is unplanned—just the stuff of life in which a precious human steps in, the good news personified.

We are called to this work, and it might not seem like much, but if you play your one note and I play mine and she plays hers, together it will create a beautiful song that sounds like freedom for the captives and good news to the poor. May the broken-hearted be healed and ashes turned to beauty in our generation.

God, make us worthy of Your calling.

CHAPTER 4

Fashion Concerns

Gather round, lambs, so I can lend both leadership and confession to some serious issues. This is no time to mess around. The following matters are grave, and we must rid our generation of these afflictions. This is how we'll be memorialized in movies and documentaries and our grandchildren's costumes during "2010s Week," so we should tighten up our legacy.

Listen, some fashion trends, captured regularly on iPhones and Buzzfeed, are assaulting our culture and must be addressed. I suspect that you, like me, are both critic and culprit; so this is a manifesto *and* a confessional. We must repent and be cleansed of the following fads.

The first is a specific tragedy I call Leggings-As-Pants/ Tights-As-Leggings (LAP/TAL = no). And don't make me delve into the crisis that is Tights-As-Pants (TAP = seek professional intervention).

Here is the caveat: Leggings-As-Pants (LAP) is permissible

if the following rule is obeyed: Your privates are covered by a shirt, sweater, or dress. Privates are heretofore understood as areas north of upper thigh and south of muffin top. I don't want to see your hinterlands. I don't want to know the shape of your underwear (or that you aren't wearing any). I can't handle this knowledge. I am just shopping at Target and feel like I've gotten to second base with you. Unless you are Jessica Alba, underwear-region is not your best zone, pet. The world is already hard; people shouldn't be forced to circumnavigate our babymakers. With a long shirt, LAP is fully acceptable and even celebrated because stretchy fabric can be godly.

Moving on to Tights-As-Leggings (TAL). Tights are a cousin to our old archenemy: pantyhose. Remember those? I could rock nude pantyhose with white flats like a boss in 1988, until I discovered pantyhose suck. So they upgraded to "tights," slightly more substantial and often labeled "opaque." But here the rubber leaves the road, good sisters. Tights are not, in fact, opaque. They can be dark, sure, but they are still made from the wispy hair of angels. In other words, they are see-through. So when an unfortunate TAL incident occurs, it means we can see through your pants. It's too much surprise flesh. I would rather you walk around in your panties so at least I know what I'm dealing with. Should you need to bend over in your TAL, it creates an exposed-crack situation that would make your mama despair. TAL is sometimes the result of actual leggings having been stretched over our thigh meat one too many times. The leggings are simply done. The fabric has disintegrated from exhaustion, and just like that, people can see your junk. Not sure about TAL?

Ask a trusted friend. Bend over for the crack test. There is no other way. This is a test of both pants and friendship.

Let's stay in this general area. I regularly commit this offense and have no plans to repent: regular underwear with workout pants. (For the purpose of this essay, "workout pants" can be worn during actual exercise or, say, just living your life because stretchy pants feel nice.) Whatever we call them—workout pants, yoga pants, I-work-from-home pants—they feature spandex because apparently some people do squats or jumping jacks or some such in them. (Other people work out in them too. . . . They work out *meaningful, important book words*, which deserves forgivable fabric also.)

Anyhow, workout pants highlight the upper and lower butt created by aforementioned underwear. Our underwear cuts across the fleshiest part of our bodies with nary a camouflage. It is called a pantyline and it is not attractive, even on Jessica. Our thick, sturdy jeans usually mask this phenomenon, but not our stretchy pants. Our stretchies tell the world, "This is the butt flesh my underwear squeezed out and downward toward my thigh, where a nice curve used to live. But now it resembles a tragic fat spill, and I've made it as visible as possible for you."

I do not plan on remedying this because I am forty and prefer containment to visual appeal. If you are behind me at the gym (okay fine, behind me at the post office), I am sincerely sorry for the optical assault. I can't give up my underwear or my stretchy pants, so we are at an impasse. Go with God.

At the writing of this essay, overalls are back. This is too painful to discuss. I beseech Thee, Lord, return them to dust by this book's printing, every last pair. My generation already suffered this blow in the '90s. The pictures live in scrapbooks and cannot be undone. I wore mine with turtlenecks, making my upper front quadrant a true calamity. It's too soon, God. The wounds are still fresh. Spare today's youth, we humbly pray.

I approach this one gently, because you are my beloved sisters, but I call to the witness stand high-waisted jeans. They were bad the first time and are now repeat offenders. (Watch early episodes of *Friends* if you need to be reminded.) I can't get behind a sixteen-inch rise. Three more inches and it's a strapless pantsuit. Heaven help if you have even a tiny pouch of belly flesh; high-rise jeans are basically a display case for your butterball. Sure, your waist looks tiny up in your rib cage, but your butt is half the length of your body. It looks like my Grandma King's backside, and all due respect to Grandma and may she rest in peace, but that is not a compliment. (Grandma, you had a great rack. We all have different strengths.)

Men don't get off scot-free. Not only women commit fashion murder. Ladies, we can't let our men wear capris, or as I call them, *manpris*. It is so stressful. There should be no midcalf-pant option for guys. Manpris confuse us; they are the ill-conceived skort for dudes ("Skirt in the front, shorts in the back!"). Just pick a lane, man. You get shorts or pants; you don't get to marry them and make a manpri baby. This is just the way of the world. Some things you don't get to have. We keep wearing your overalls and look where that got us.

I have feelings about men's tank tops with frockets, but we should move on.

Let's discuss our children. I live in Austin, Land of Hipsters, so I know of which I speak. (I skirt this society as an owner of ironic glasses, multiple tattoos, vintage records, and Mason jars, so indulge this minor hypocrisy.) I'm all for cutely dressed children. I am. But the kids in Austin's parks look like miniature Anthropologie ads with a side of inner torment. Seven-year-olds do not need chunky infinity scarves as fashion accessories here, since our city basically oscillates between summer and less-summer.

Hand to the heavens, I saw one boy sporting a popped collar and ascot, and I pictured him at the club with his mother: *"Ashby, be a darling and pour me a spot of Bourbon while Daddy brings the yacht around."* Poor Ashby. His ascot won't withstand this filthy playground, and those things take a month to special order.

I'm just saying there is a place for Garanimals, folks. Sometimes kids need to wear jean shorts and T-shirts because, well, they are children, not performance art installations. (Unless the piece is entitled *Overstimulated Child Rips Dress on Playground Slide, Spills Gatorade Down Shirt, and Pees Pants: Childhood Fashion in Three Acts.*) We probably need fewer fedoras on third-graders with Brazilian blowouts. Let's just simmer down a bit.

I'll close by apologizing for my personal faux pas, including overaccessorizing (the only thing better than one bracelet is seven), egregious overuse of the topknot, wearing necklaces to make T-shirts "dressy," and an inappropriate utilization of flip-flops. And of course the underwear/stretchy pants conundrum.

Okay fine, I also overaccessorized my babies, as an infant girl probably did not require elaborate hair paraphernalia, earrings, layered tulle skirts, striped kneesocks, and Mary Janes.

But I've never let Brandon out in manpris, so you're welcome, world.

CHAPTER 5

Run Your Race

I refuse to be shamed by this: I love *American Idol*. Thirteen seasons in and I still dedicate DVR space to it every week. I don't even care, you guys. My musician friends are all, "It harms the integrity of creative license and fabricates a fan base that makes true artisanship something something," and other words come out of their mouths and I'm like, "YOU ARE NOT MY BOSS!"

Week after week, okay fine, year after year I sit on my couch and grin at the TV. Then I pull up my favorite performances of the night and grin at my laptop. Then they win or lose and I cry and they hug their parents and I sob and they are amazing and I get choked up. Every week.

I am proud of them.

I am inspired by people doing what they do best.

Gosh, we were just born to do stuff, weren't we? God truly built gifts into our lives. Everyone is good at something. Some make a living with their gifts and others just bless the world.

I am thinking of several women who are really, really good at friendship. They are such spectacular friends to me that it isn't even fair. And others whom I constantly admire for being such good moms. Two friends threw creative, fun, adorable parties for their daughters last weekend, and I was in awe because I am not a Fun Party Mom. (I just do not have this particular gear, but when I witness it, I'm all, "Well done!" and "Thank you for inviting Remy so she can have some childhood memories of fun parties and maybe time will dull her recollection and she'll think I threw some.")

I don't like when people minimize their gifts. There is a difference between humility and insecurity, and self-effacement does no one any favors. We teach our watching children to doubt and excuse and diminish themselves. Do we want our kids to reflect on their mothers and have absolutely no idea what we loved? What we were good at? What got our pulses racing and minds spinning? Don't we want them to see us doing what we do best?

My mom went back to college when she had four kids in high school, middle school, and elementary school, and it has always been a source of pride for me. She was a teacher in her heart and needed the degree to match, so she chased the dream long before it was convenient or well-timed or easy. Yes, she fell off the oat bran wagon (kindly recall 1990) and we got store-bought prom dresses, but we watched her fly. It never occurred to us to settle for less.

What are you good at? Not sure? What do people constantly say you are good at? Others usually identify our gifts long before we do. Maybe you have career material. In most cases, someone will pay you to do what you love. You might have a job you hate, doing work you don't care about, and you are stuck in inertia. Is there a job description with your name on it?

Do you know that I always, my entire life, loved to write but never dared imagine it could be a job? I taught elementary school, one of the noblest professions, but I wasn't great and felt trapped. I later stayed home with the babies I had every other summer, and when the youngest turned two, I told Brandon, "According to our schedule, I'm due for another newborn this summer, so I'm going to birth a different kind." And I wrote my first book. Obviously writing a book no one asked for with three kids under five is an Insane Person Choice, but sometimes you throw out logic and run your race.

Do you know what else? I thought humor was one of my throwaway qualities forever. Surely that had no place in Jesus Work. Frankly, I considered it a liability—as if I should overcome it and get serious, for the love. (What kind of a Bible teacher loves Will Ferrell?) I figured I should manage the important stuff and ratchet down the humor, because I am a grown woman who works for Jesus. But guess what? God created an entire package. It all counts. There are no throwaway qualities. In fact, those qualities might point you in just the right direction. Nothing is wasted: not a characteristic, preference, experience, tragedy, quirk, nothing. It is all you and it is all purposed and it can all be used for great and glorious good.

Maybe your best thing won't draw a paycheck, but it is how you shine and glow and come to life and bless the world. May

I legitimize your gifts? Just because you don't get a pay stub doesn't mean you shrink back or play small or give it all up. Do your thing. Play your note. We are all watching and learning, moved. You are making the world kinder, more beautiful, wiser, funnier, richer, better. Give your gifts the same attention you would if it paid. (Or paid well! Some do our best, most meaningful work for peanuts. Don't be shamed out of your race for a bigger paycheck. I didn't make a living as a writer for years. My neighbor, upon hearing I was a Christian author, once said: "Oh! Is there a market for that?" Me: "I have no idea.")

Run your race.

Maybe you need to invest in your gifts. Take a class. Go to a conference. Sign up for a seminar. Start that small business. Put that website up. Build in some space. Say yes to that thing. Work with a mentor. Stop minimizing what you are good at and throw yourself into it with no apologies. Do you know who will do this for you? *No one. You are it.* Don't bury that talent, because the only thing fear yields is one dormant gift in a shallow grave.

How many trot out that tired cliché—"I'm waiting for God to open a door"—and He is all, "I love you, but get going, pumpkin, because usually chasing the dream in your heart looks surprisingly like work. Don't just stand there, bust a move." (God often sounds like Young MC.) You are good at something for a reason. God designed you this way, on purpose. It isn't fake or a fluke or small. These are the mind and heart and hands and voice you've been given, so use them.

Let the rest of us grin at you while you run your race. Let us be proud. Let us be inspired and grateful that God made you to do this thing like a boss. The timing is never right. Forget that. It rarely just falls into your lap. You are probably not guaranteed success. This might be a risk. It will require sacrifices from you and maybe your people, and you might step out on shaky, shaky legs. But off you go because we were not created to stand still, even though that is safe and familiar and you are guaranteed never to fall or stumble or grow weary.

We were made to run.

RUN.

I'm grinning at you. We all are.

CHAPTER 6

Not Buying

I just saw a commercial for mousse that will not only battle this Texas humidity and make me a hair model but also make people laugh hysterically at my wit! *Who knew I could be that funny?* It seems my new hair will attract young, good-looking, multicultural friends, and we will run through a field laughing over our shoulders while our hair bounces and shines.

Well done, mousse!

I have some tips for advertisers. Locked away in your labs, you forget about regular consumers in the real world, but I'm here to remedy that. We want you to know our brains are actually functional, and furthermore, we have a decent grasp on the English language, including made-up words that aren't actually a thing.

Yes, some of us are getting older. I know. Fine. True. You're onto us. However, when you peddle products with invented words like *collagen modules* and *liposome spheres*, you give us angry feelings. When you promise your "synthesized skin-identical ceramides will visibly turn back the hands of time on skin damage," did you account for the tanning oil I put on my teenaged face and how I refused hats to avoid an irregular tan? Am I to believe you can reverse decades of solar tomfoolery? *With your ceramides?* Stop it. Unless you have a time-traveling DeLorean, these wrinkles and sunspots are here to stay.

Another thing. Regarding your celebrity endorsers: The day Jennifer Lopez styles her hair with L'Oreal EverSleek and Halle Barry coats her eyelashes with Maybelline will be the day magazines stop casting twenty-two-year-old models in antiaging ads ("The only thing that will help this college student fight the evils of aging more than our expensive cream is her PHYSICAL AND BIOLOGICAL YOUTH!"). This is horsecrappery.

Advertisers, we know these wealthy, famous women have aestheticians and masseuses on their permanent payroll, so they are not fetching their beauty products from Walgreens. We know Sarah Jessica Parker's hair is not Garnier Nutrisse Natural Shades #60 Light Natural Brown. We would rather you admitted, "Eva Mendez doesn't actually use our lip gloss, but we've included a picture of her in our advertisement because she thinks fondly of you while her lips are being injected with the blood pigment of fairy babies."

Listen, just talk real to us. We might actually believe it if you said, "This product will neither enhance your chakras nor transform your troubled relationships, but it will mostly remove hard water stains in your bathtub. That's the best we can do here." Super. Even better? If you cast a tired-looking mom with dirty hair and torn yoga pants to scrub the tub with an expression that makes sense rather than a coiffed lady in linen capri pants who smiles at this fascinating experience. I have never in my life been delighted while scrubbing my shower. I hope this gets through to you.

Inversely, Creators of As-Seen-On-TV Products, you can probably tamp down the utter defeat your actors experience during ordinary tasks like using the remote control with their arms under a blanket (#thestruggleisreal) or slicing a tomato. These challenges are not incapacitating an entire generation like your market researchers have led you to believe. "Chopping vegetables the old way" doesn't actually "take forever," and I'm not sure "eliminating cooking's most frustrating task with the innovative EZ Egg Cracker" has gauged the average cook's ability to crack an egg without a nervous breakdown. I'm just saying your ads are high on drama and low on felt needs.

Maybe the As-Seen-On-TV people should just market to celebrity endorsers and skip us altogether, because they have real troubles. Why, just recently Gwyneth lamented the age-old frustration with Parisian concierges: "When you go to Paris and your concierge sends you to some restaurant because they get a kickback, it's like, 'No. Where should I really be? Where is the great bar with organic wine? Where do I get a bikini wax in Paris?'"[1]

Bless.

Hey sisters, may I inject some opinions here? Advertising aimed at women is a disaster. On one hand, they bombard us with a not-so-subtle message: "You are getting older and this is the worst thing that ever happened." According to the beauty industry, with the right purchases (wink) we can reclaim our youth, fix our pathetic baby-bearing bodies, and fool everyone! Forget how the images they offer are absolute works of fiction. They sell carica-tures, and even as our minds acknowledge the deception, our hands reach for our wallets. We believe their assessment.

"You are not beautiful enough, but we can fix it."

This same industry believes real life is also too hard for us, but they are here to help. Most notably, the food business. I mean, apparently we cannot possibly cook like every generation before us in history. Advertisers suggest a good breakfast is utterly beyond us. Crack an egg? How could we possibly? We can't man-age real food in the morning! Help us, Marketing People! Give us something fast! Help us through this difficult conundrum of breakfast with food-things you concocted in your labs!

Meanwhile, it takes three minutes to fry an egg and serve it over toast.

We should stop listening to this nonsense. Women have nurtured their families with good, real food since creation. It simply isn't true that cooking is beyond our capacity. To feed the machine, advertisers use buzzwords like *quick and easy*, *no-fuss*, *ready in minutes*, *heat and serve*. But do we even want those qualities around our tables? When did chopping onions and peeling carrots become so abhorrent? Isn't that how women have fed their people all along? With stuff that came from the actual earth?

I don't like the picture marketers paint of us—overly busy moms with no time or energy to feed our families well. I don't appreciate how cooking is portrayed as an unbearable imposition, a hassle better left to professionals. I certainly don't like their options comprised of absolute food fiction. (Lean Pockets are not actually a "healthy alternative.")

This is crazy. Cooking is not an affliction, and we aren't incapable women who can't crack eggs. We should disregard those commercials and remember that feeding people real food has always been a good, noble task. Nothing unclenches my shoulders more than turning on some Ben Howard music, pouring a glass of Cabernet, and starting dinner. Just drop some onion and garlic in olive oil, and your day improves exponentially. Cooking isn't actually hard at all. It is the simple mechanism that nourished every generation in time.

Messages that tell us we aren't pretty enough, young enough, thin enough, or desirable enough are garbage. Anyone who implies we are unable to care for our own families is lying. If you believe the persona that marketing culture has crafted— helpless, too stressed, overwhelmed, incompetent (without their products)—I am here to say otherwise. You are not a moron or a damsel in distress. You are smart and able, and getting older is not a tragedy. Don't believe them. Even if some observations are descriptive, they need not be prescriptive.

You are not a total hot disaster! Well, no more than any of us. You can do hard things. (Some "hard things" are actually "easy things" rebranded as impossible.) You are more than some company's profitability, and you don't need their tricks to live a beautiful, meaningful life. We can reclaim our merit without dancing like monkeys.

But just in case, I have one inch of gray hair, lovely readers, so I'm off to color my hair with a boxed dye, which will have stunning and otherworldly results, because Cameron Diaz uses the exact same brand.

Not only can you do hard things, but also you can make fancy sounding French food! I give you an absolute foolproof recipe (adapted from Ina Garten):

Cᴑ

Beef Bourguignon
Serves 6–8

To begin, you'll need:

1 T. olive oil

8 oz. bacon, diced

2 1/2 lbs. chuck beef cut into one-inch cubes

Kosher salt

Freshly ground black pepper

1 lb. carrots, sliced diagonally into one-inch chunks

2 yellow onions, sliced

2 tsp. chopped garlic

1 bottle dry red wine (like a Pinot Noir)

1 can (2 cups) beef broth

1 T. tomato paste

1 tsp. fresh thyme leaves (or 1/2 teaspoon dried)

4 T. unsalted butter at room temperature

3 T. all-purpose flour

1 lb. fresh mushrooms, thickly sliced

For serving, you'll need:

Country bread or Sour Dough, toasted or grilled and rubbed
   with garlic clove

1/2 cup chopped fresh parsley

First of all, don't panic at the ingredient list. Look at it: butter and flour and such. You have almost all of this. Don't let the fancy name fool you: This is basically stew. A one-pot meal, sisters. So get your Dutch oven because you are about to make magic.

Preheat the oven to 350 degrees.

Heat olive oil in a Dutch oven. Add bacon (baaaaacooooon!) and cook over medium about ten minutes, stirring a bit until it is brown. Remove with a slotted spoon to a large plate (but leave that baaaaacooooon grease in the pot, for the love of deliciousness).

Dry the beef cubes with a paper towel and give them a hefty douse of salt and pepper. In single layer batches, sear the beef cubes on all four sides in the hot-oil-slash-bacon-grease (about three to five minutes). Remove the cubes to the plate with the bacon and keep this up until all of the beef is browned. (Don't skip this step! Sure, it adds a few minutes to the recipe but it will turn that cheap cut of meat into a superstar later. Stop rushing. What else do you need to do? Go cure cancer?)

Into all that good juice and drippings, toss in the carrots, onions, a tablespoon of salt, and two teaspoons of pepper. Cook for ten to fifteen minutes, stirring occasionally. Add the garlic and cook for another minute. (At this point, the aroma gets ridiculous.) Put the meat and bacon back in the pot. Add the bottle of wine (you read that right . . . the entire bottle, you lushes!) plus enough beef broth to cover the meat. Add the tomato paste and thyme. Bring to a simmer, cover the pot with a lid, and slide in the oven for about two hours until the meat and vegetables are fork-tender.

Pray someone knocks on your door to witness how good your house smells.

Back on the stovetop, combine two tablespoons of butter and the flour with a fork. Stir the product into the stew (this will thicken it and add creaminess). Sauté the mushrooms in two more tablespoons of butter until lightly browned, and add to the stew. Bring to a boil, then lower the heat and simmer for fifteen minutes. Season to taste.

To serve, toast thick slices of bread, then rub them with a cut clove of garlic. The garlic melts into the hot bread like magic. For each serving, spoon the stew over a slice of bread and sprinkle with parsley. (You could also serve over mashed potatoes or egg noodles or just *nothing* because it is so delectable, but whatever you do, dunk some bread in it.)

Serve in shallow bowls with a rich, spicy Cabernet, and a fire in the fireplace.

This is such a crowd-pleaser, you have no idea. You cannot mess this up. If this is for company, make it the day before and heat to serve, because the first day of this recipe is divine, but on its second day you hear angels sing and see the face of the Lord.

CHAPTER 7

Tell the Truth

A few weeks ago, I was on a plane. Specifically, I was fretting on a plane. Our little HGTV show was premiering soon, and I was having an internal crisis for a myriad of reasons: *Our family will be exposed on a whole 'nother level. Should we have accepted this remodel? Will my readers find it excessive? Did we represent God well? Will this make me the next media target? Is it okay to live in such a cute house after writing 7? Did we make the right choice? How are people going to react to this?*

My brain had some ideas. It suggested acting assured and self-confident when talking about the show publicly. My brain told me to craft careful messaging and hold my cards close. *Be easy breezy!* it said. *Don't let anyone know you are conflicted, for Pete's sake. Do not provide ammunition for the Internet to use against you. There is no room here for personal struggle; if you are having a branding crisis, zip it. It is too late for this nonsense.*

I stared out the window, writing press releases in my head

to shape this correctly, when a clear and immediate thought slammed into my brain.

Just tell the truth.

It was so right and simple, tears drained down my face. *Just tell the truth, Jen. If you are conflicted and worry a renovation might muddy the message of 7, just say it. If you are afraid people will be disappointed in the show, admit that. If you're scared new people won't like you and might be mean, fess up. If you are mostly sure you made the right decision but have some doubts, concede it. It's okay to have human feelings, even if a whole big bunch of people are watching you have them.*

I'm not prone to exaggeration (I am exactly prone to exaggeration), but before that flight landed, it had become my new mantra for life: Just tell the truth. Whatever question comes, just tell the truth. If you don't know the answer, admit you struggle. If you disagree with the conversation, don't sit there acting otherwise. Stop trying to self-preserve; that is a fool's errand.

Sisters, can you imagine a world where we could be free enough to tell the truth? Letting hard things be hard and confusing things be confusing? If we fought the instinct to prop things up, to polish and tilt and arrange the pieces in just the right lighting, we would be free. We could all exhale.

The best I offer the world is the truth—my highest gift. What the world does with it is not up to me. I am not in charge of outcomes, opinions, assessments. I am not in the business of damage control. When I present a fabricated version of myself—the self who knows all, is ever certain, always steps strong—we all lose, because I cannot keep up with that lie and neither can you.

Here is the truth: Sometimes life is complicated. Do you know how often I make decisions that seem mostly right, but then a few weird slivers remain and I move anyway? Do you know how much theology I have to leave in the "I just won't understand this until I meet Him face-to-face" drawer? I deeply want to live well but constantly worry some of my categories are in full disarray. Sometimes I'm not sure. Sometimes I'm conflicted. Sometimes I change my mind. Sometimes I'm way more human than folks are comfortable with.

We all are. That's the irony of it. Why do we think others live carefree, self-assured lives while we slink around in the messy middle? Doubt is universal; read the Bible. Life is plagued with regret, confusion, uncertainty, and colossal failures. Scratch just beneath the surface and you'll find humanity in all of us.

If we could believe we are deeply connected in the fragile places, we could drop the games. When you tell me the truth about yourself, I no longer hide from you. You become safe for me. So guess what? You are now a recipient of my truth too. I am drawn to you. Your vulnerability makes a path for my own. Your truth-telling says to me, "I will not despise, judge, or abandon you." Ironically, it gives me the courage to be afraid, the strength to be weak.

What keeps you from telling the truth? I'm guessing shame and fear, those two devils. The doggone irony is how they often prey upon an imagined reaction. People *might* get mad. They *might* be ugly. They *might* talk bad about me. They *might* not understand. We invent a worst-case scenario and it mutes us.

The truth is, most people respect vulnerability and hold it with tender hands, especially those who love us and faithfully bear our stories. We are so afraid, but truth-telling leads to life. Like Brené Brown said in *Daring Greatly* (put this book down immediately and buy hers):

> Daring greatly is not about winning or losing. It's about courage. In a world where scarcity and shame dominate and feeling afraid has become second nature, vulnerability is subversive. Uncomfortable. It's even a little dangerous at times . . . [But] nothing is as uncomfortable, dangerous, and hurtful as believing that I'm standing on the outside of my life looking in and wondering what it would be like if I had the courage to show up and let myself be seen.[1]

And even if someone is nasty, recognize the safe people who guard your story. They deserve to be in your stable and be trusted with your truth. As for the others? As Scott Stratten, author of *UnMarketing* says: "Don't try to win over the haters; you're not the jackass whisperer."[2] (I will now abuse this phrase with reckless abandon.)

That brings us to the other side, dear ones: receiving someone else's truth. Has it ever been scarier to risk vulnerability? The Internet is terrifying. Christians, specifically, can be petrifying. I've watched good people put truthful, hard words out there and get slaughtered. Every time that happens, people retreat more, because who wants that sort of humiliation? Brown has more to say:

We judge people in areas where we're vulnerable to shame, especially picking folks who are doing worse than we're doing. If I feel good about my parenting, I have no interest in judging other people's choices. If I feel good about my body, I don't go around making fun of other people's weight or appearance. We're hard on each other because we're using each other as a launching pad out of our own perceived shaming deficiency.[3]

May I suggest a starting place as truth receivers? It is okay for someone else to struggle. Furthermore, it is okay to not fix it/solve it/answer it/discredit it. Another believer can experience tension, say something true that makes people uncomfortable, and God will not fall off His throne. It is not our responsibility to fix every mess. If someone steps onto the scary ledge of truth, it is enough to acknowledge her courage and make this promise: *I am here with you as your friend, not your Savior.* We are not good gods over one another; we are better humans beside each other.

Simply speaking truth out loud is healing in and of itself. When people courageously voice a true, hard thing, they've already stolen some of its dark power before we offer one word to fix it. Theology backs that up. Of our own Jesus, Scripture says, "In him was life, and that life was the light of all mankind. The light shines in the darkness, and the darkness has not overcome it" (John 1:4–5).

Life and light are greater than the darkness.

Pulling something difficult from its dark hiding place and into the light is innately healing. When we bear witness to this bravery, we should simply receive it gratefully, knowing the heavy lifting is already done.

It is good to remember in community, and even better to practice individually, that light trumps darkness. If you're concealing a dark struggle, you guarantee its power if it's shrouded in secrecy. Buried, it is free to hinder you, grow in your imagination, and truncate your future. It can hold you back, destroy relationships, and break your spirit. It can absolutely wreak havoc on your authenticity, as the inside contradicts the outside day after day, month after month. Secrets are wild and free in the dark.

But when you drag that truth kicking and screaming into the glorious light, you can see it for what it is. It wasn't as menacing as it pretended. It isn't as uncommon as it claimed. It is actually sad and pathetic sitting there in the light, shriveling up and losing power over you. You said it out loud and no one dropped dead, so what can it still hold over you?

Then your good people blast their light on it, shining truth and love and compassion and understanding, and it withers even more. With every *I am here* and *I've been there* and *You aren't alone* and *God has this*, your scary truth gets less terrifying, less overwhelming, less paralyzing. It becomes fully exposed with no secrets left to threaten you. You are 2 Corinthians 4, because although this darkness pressed you so hard, it did not crush you. Perhaps it struck you down, but look at you: You are not destroyed. You see that in the light. You are still standing. If you are still breathing, there is still hope.

Then what a rescue—Jesus shines His light onto your dark

truth and you are saved. "For God, who said, 'Let light shine out of darkness,' made his light shine in our hearts to give us the light of the knowledge of God's glory displayed in the face of Christ" (2 Cor. 4:6). In the Rolodex of privileges as one of God's own, certainly our status as overcomers is one of the highest. Because greater is He that is in us than he that is in the world. This isn't just pretty poetry; it is the gospel truth.

The darkness has not overcome the light, and the light is ours.

Just tell the truth because it sets us free. This first domino unleashes a chain reaction of liberation. If we tell truth in the small things, our honesty is well-practiced when stuff gets dire. This creates a sincere community for which the earth is starving. In a world full of the fake, artificial, pretend, and superficial, we have the sustenance to nourish our starving hearts.

I promise to be gentle with your truth-telling, and you've already demonstrated tenderness with mine. And as we witness this beautiful community, we aren't just observing vulnerability but rather chains breaking, darkness receding, victory rising. We are watching the light win truth by truth, and when enough bright places are created, the dark has nowhere else to hide.

Show up. Be seen. Tell the truth. Be free.

CHAPTER 8

Thank-You Notes (Part 1)

Jimmy Fallon is the best thing to happen to late-night television since Netflix. He is shamelessly awkward; and if I could, I would cut a lock of his hair. My favorite segment is "Thank-You Notes," in which he expresses sarcastic gratitude to various and sundry things. If imitation is the sincerest form of flattery, this is probably closer to outright plagiarism. I offer the following Thank-You Notes scattered throughout this book, like comic relief segments, written with help from my hilarious Facebook friends.

❧

Thank you, Spanx. Because of you, my postbaby body can mold like Jell-O into a svelte, sexy little shape . . . for a few hours anyway. Your ability to lift and tuck simply takes my breath away, literally! May you continue to do God's work and be the progenitor of the muffin top. THANK YOU, SARA BLAKELY!! Sincerely, All Women.

Thank you, Daylight Savings Time, for making people wax on about the wonder of an extra hour of sleep, only to serve as an especially depressing reminder to parents that kids don't care about farmers and harvests and extra hours of daylight. I enjoy my kids standing at my bedside at 4:30 a.m. like creepy, wide-awake Children of the Corn. Naptimes are also jacked, so there's that. With all due respect-ish, A Tired Mom.

Thank you, Obvious Warning Labels. Without you I might have stuck my kid in a washing machine, lit a match near an open gas line, used my hair dryer while sleeping, or, God forbid, not realized eggs may contain—wait for it—eggs. I have no idea how I ever function without you. (I almost ingested the contents of a lava lamp just yesterday, but your label made another quick save. God bless.)

Thank you, Instagram Filters, for you have helped me put out many works of photographic fiction that make me appear younger, tanner, and thinner than I actually am. Natural lighting may be my nemesis, but Lo-Fi is my BFF. LYLAS.

Thank you, Daylight and Rearview Mirror, for bringing to light the long, wiry chin hairs I missed during my morning tweeze session. You also exposed my eyebrows as an absolute tragedy. I have enough undetected facial hair to qualify me as a Sasquatch, so thanks for the heads-up. (Sorry, Car Next to Me at the Stoplight, there is no other way.)

Thank you, Retail Stores, for putting Christmas decorations out in October. It is not even Halloween and my children have morphed into unbridled capitalists. Now every commercial is an excuse for my children to scream, "I want that for Christmas!" For three months. What a delight. Sincerely, Mom Trying to Teach Her Children About Baby Jesus but Struggling to Compete with a Disney-Themed Slanket.

Thank you, Amazon Prime, first, for existing. Secondly, for allowing me to make "free shipping" the justification for buying all the books and only seeing how much I saved. Thirdly, for allowing me to purchase boys' underwear, fish sauce, toilet paper, and folders with brads without leaving my couch. And for shipping these items to me in four different boxes, none properly sized for the item it contains. You've made this lazy antishopper so happy. Be my boyfriend, AP.

Thank you, Maxi Dresses, for helping me appear dressed up, as though I really made an effort, but making me feel as if I'm wearing a nightgown out in public. You are basically crotchless yoga pants, and I salute you.

Thank you, Period Calendar App, for warnings to tread lightly around affected wife for three days a month. You've also helped him learn to not say, "Could this be your period talking?" because that is his one-way ticket to see the face of crazy. Sincerely, Wife of a Husband.

Thank you, Four-Year-Old, for keeping my vanity in check with constant reminders about my "fat tummy" and "old skin." These tragic conditions are your doing, but I appreciate your keen powers of observation. I can't be walking around acting like Gisele when I have important things to attend to, like cooking a meal for you to hate. Sincerely, Your Old Fat Mom.

Thank you, Netflix, for the fifteen seconds between episodes to decide if I'm going to do anything with my life today. The answer is inevitably no, but nobody can say you didn't give me the option.

Thank you, 4:00 p.m., for being the time of day that thoroughly confuses me: post-homework and pre-dinner. I am already exhausted and fairly irritable. The children are losing their ever-loving minds, and husband is still tucked away in his sane office with all mental faculties intact and won't answer my SOS texts to *hurry and come home or their blood is on your hands.* Do I make a coffee? Or pour a glass of wine? Yours, Witching-Hour Survivor.

Thank you, Coffee. For everything. You make life possible. I don't want to make you feel weird, but you are my soul mate. Well done.

Thank you, Gym Childcare, for giving me the opportunity to watch TV, take a shower by myself, and drink a smoothie while reading a magazine. Oh! And work out too, but let's be honest, that's not the main reason I'm there. (And did I once check in my offspring, then scoot next door for sushi? Just let it go. YOU DON'T KNOW MY LIFE.)

Thank you, Miss "Could you bring me these pants in a size 2?" for finding the dressing room adjacent to mine no matter when or where I try on clothes. You keep me humble. I also appreciate hearing how my size shirt "swallows you." And yes, we all know how "cold you are in here" without any natural insulation. Eat a sandwich.

ALL THESE
PEOPLE WHO LIVE
IN YOUR HOUSE

CHAPTER 9

Hope for Spicy Families

Although it's reductive, I categorize most families as either "sweet" or "spicy." There are pros and cons to both, with tons of overlap on the Venn diagram, but still. In general, a family trends toward one or the other.

One guess which way the Hatmakers lean.

We are spicy people. We love obnoxious humor and sarcasm and are very, very loud. The lot of us suffers from Enormous Feelings, which makes us a passionate, emotional bunch. Our permanent default setting is exclamation marks!! We don't really "do gentle." We don't actually know what that means.

So anytime I am around a sweet family, I have a crisis. It simmers until a comment from one of their children to another—"*Sister? Would you like the last brownie? You take it since you did all my chores as a surprise for my half birthday...*"—launches a watershed moment. Brandon knows this about me and has weathered the reentry numerous times:

ME: What is wrong with us? We need a new system for people to talk nicer in this house. We are raising feral children! Why don't any of our kids knit? We need to quit raising our voices FOR THE REST OF OUR LIVES or we are doomed. Our kids are probably going to kill people one day. They are on dark paths to incarceration or street violence!

BRANDON: Street violence here in the suburbs?

ME: THERE COULD BE VIOLENCE IN THESE STREETS—we're near the end times! We need to figure out how to be more adorable! Our kids don't even know any hymns! How will we break out in spontaneous family worship? WWAVD? (What would Ann Voskamp do?) Let's just throw in the towel.

Nothing makes me diagnose my family as "catastrophic" quicker than another family behaving—a terrible comparison game that isn't even fair, as I'm not privy to their atmosphere beyond that one hour. Maybe that darling brownie-deferring sister gave the other a roundhouse kick to the temple the next day for calling her a *turd burger*. We don't know these things, and it's easy to reduce another family to a prototype to compare against our undomesticated family. The result is despair, then certainty that our children are ruined.

Is there any worry like parent worry? We are responsible for whole human lives here. *This is it.* This is their one childhood leading to one adulthood. They absorb all the hours in this home, emulating what they've seen, GOD HELP US. Every mother I know worries she isn't doing this right, failing in countless ways, seen and unseen. Our family faults seem so egregious, omissions and breakdowns and missteps that constitute a complete and total disaster.

I heard recently, "If you are worried about being a bad parent, you are probably a good one."

I wanted to believe this so badly. Am I? Am I a good mom? Because I mostly feel like I'm spitting into the wind here. Then something happened. I jumped outside my mind where the crazy lives and watched myself talking to my kids. I was so nice sometimes! I said sweet and precious things here and there! There were so many *I love yous* and *You are very smarts* and attentive *Mmhmmms* and *Sounds awesomes* and *Great job on thats* laced through. I watched myself be a good parent and realized I am my own worst critic and sometimes even a liar, convincing myself that nothing good is happening and it's all my fault, or maybe Brandon's fault, and the kids are horrid and we are a disaster.

I should ignore myself more often.

Why do we exaggerate our failures and ignore our successes? I would never overvalue another mother's lows and neglect her triumphs, so why would I do that to myself? Why do any of us? We observe other parents' strengths with 20/20 vision while our strengths are blurred. I declare your goodness as easily as I affirm my wretchedness; they are inversely proportional. I am conditioned to minimize your humanity and overemphasize mine.

Whether you are a sweet mama imagining how the spicy mamas have all the fun (not true: we're mostly breaking up fights), or a spicy mama assuming the sweet mamas have all the tenderness (they don't: they are mostly, um, I'm not actually sure, I've never been in a sweet family): if you are worried about being a bad parent, you are probably a good one.

Some of the good is obvious, the stuff we readily notice in others—the loving words, the endless attention, the eye contact, the praise. We read to our kids and tuck them in with kisses and use affirming parenting language and attend all the games/recitals/tournaments/programs. We braid hair and tie ribbons and apply Band-Aids and pretend our kids' art is pretty. We do all that, and it is good, and it counts.

Some of the good is less obvious, the stuff that also happens in every home—the apologies, the conflict resolution, the tough love, the boundaries, the making up, the hard lessons. We are molding failure into character, both our kids' and ours. Every parent blows it. Every kid comes unhinged. Every family goes off the rails. That doesn't mean we are ruined; it means we are ordinary. Course correction is standard. These moments often feel bad because they started bad, but they are actually good, and they count too.

This is my point: You are doing a better job than you think. Self-criticism sometimes improves best practices, but it can also lie to you and probably has. You may need to ignore your mind and watch yourself awhile—not just detecting the sharp moments but the soft ones, for I assure you they are there. If you would tell a friend having a bad mom day, "It's okay! Your kids know you love them. Everyone loses it sometimes. Parenting is hard. Tomorrow is a new day . . . ," then you should extend that same compassion to yourself.

Listen, motherhood is not Knitting While Singing Hymns all the time. If that's our standard and every deviation produces a guilt trip, we are doomed. Not every moment is big-ticket. Not every conversation with kids is esteem-building. Sometimes they just need to get in the bathtub and stop stalling. There is no shame in that. Motherhood has many slivers. Sure, sometimes we "intentionally parent" (quotation marks in honor of my mom, who says she and her friends just raised us but people of my generation "parent"), but we also manage, discipline, intervene, boss around, implement, and even just survive sometimes. We wear many hats and they don't all include The Precious Feels. We don't live in an after-school special; we're running households here.

Condemnation is a trick of the enemy, not the language of the heavens. Shame is not God's tool, so if we are slaves to it, we're way off the beaten path. And it is harsh out there, debilitating actually. If your inner monologue is critical, endlessly degrading, it's time to move back to grace. Then we can breathe and assess our own parenting with the same kindness we extend to others. Only our overly critical, overly involved generation could engineer such carefully curated childhood environments and still declare ourselves failures. We are loving, capable mothers reading the room all wrong.

Can I tell you my goal for my kids? That their childhood is mostly good. People, I declare "mostly good" a raging success. If I am mostly patient and they are mostly obedient, great. If we are mostly nurturing and they turn out mostly well-adjusted, super. Every childhood needs a portion of lame, boring, aggravating, and tedious. Good grief, life is not a Nickelodeon set. They need *something* to gripe about one day.

"Mostly good" is later remembered as "loved and safe." I now label my childhood "magical" though Mom slapped me across the face when I was in seventh grade and never bought me Guess jeans and accidentally left me at church several times. Mostly good is enough. Mostly good produces healthy kids who know they are valued and either forget the other parts or turn them into funny stories.

You are doing a wonderful job. Parenting is mind-numbingly hard and no one is perfect at it and we'll all jack a thousand parts, yet somehow, against all odds, it will be enough.

And if stepping outside your mind to self-observe or planting your feet on a grace highway doesn't work, come to my house for one afternoon and be guaranteed to feel better about your family, as you may recall how I told my then fifth-grader, after sassing off, to get a shovel, go in the backyard, and dig his own grave.

Because *that* is WJHWD.

CHAPTER 10

Surviving School

I recently completed the marathon called Getting Five Children Ready for Back to School, and now I need therapy. I spent around 400 million dollars, drove to a dozen stores, and almost became a serial killer over folders with brads. The kids have gym shoes, regular shoes, new clothes, new backpacks, lunch boxes, and school supplies out the yin-yang; we've been to back-to-school night, orientation, schedule pickup, and freshman camp; I filled out personality inventories, insurance documents, volunteer forms, registration packets, and parent contracts; we've had haircuts, vaccinations, eye exams, pep talks, bike tune-ups, and meltdowns. The refrigerator was stocked. The pantry was filled. The lunch accounts were updated. The lectures were given. On the first day of school, the kids were photographed at home and with teachers because humiliation is an important part of childhood.

It will take an entire calendar year to recover so I can do it again.

I was born in 1974, gentle reader. May I tell you what I remember of back-to-school? Let's see, one new pair of corduroys, a homemade bangs trim (disastrous), and some hand-me-downs from our babysitter. We rode the bus on the first day of school and I don't remember how we found our class, because not one mother was on the campus (they were already at Jazzercise). We brought one notebook, a pencil, and a bologna sandwich in last year's lunch box. The end.

Furthermore, do you know how often my mom volunteered in my classroom? Zero times. I cannot remember any mother ever at my school. My mom did not have Parent Homework, and our science fair projects looked like garbage because we did them ourselves as sloppy, prepubescent students whose parents weren't about to interrupt *Dynasty* to determine what kind of soil is best for plant growth. There were no parent-led school carnivals, book fairs, or fall festivals, because our parents worked—and ain't nobody had time for a sand art booth.

It was a totally different time. The parents and teachers were in charge, and children were not the little rulers. If my teacher called because I was acting like a lunatic, my parents believed her (*I know, right?*) and made sure I would think twice before opening my smart mouth again. Sidebar: Teachers, I wish parents understood that their precious child probably isn't an innocent victim of your "daddy issues and rage disorder." And Mom, your daughter got detention for an actual reason. Kaitlyn-Grace needs to do her homework and stop sassing. Her tears are manufactured. Kaitlyn-Grace should join theater.

Back in the day, the world did not revolve around us, and

when we blew it in school, we paid the piper. Teachers were not expected to sprinkle all the Precious Snowflakes with magical fairy dust every day, and parents were not expected to repeat all their years of schooling with a daily homework avalanche. (I have been in third grade six times and I am d-o-n-e.)

Getting children through school is now like completing a doctoral program. I absolutely understand why moms claim "less work" as a reason to homeschool. I have no idea how parents with traditional jobs manage it. How do teachers who are also parents do it? I work from home with a flexible schedule, but if I got home at 6:00 p.m. and still faced homework (never mind the whole dinner, quality time, and bedtime routine), I would be rocking in a corner in the fetal position.

In my opinion, we need to ratchet it down. Moms, I can barely speak of what Pinterest has done to us here. Between bento boxes with sandwiches cut into the shape of dolphins leaping into a sea of kale, and spraying our kids' feet with lemon essential oils to soothe their troubles, I just can't even . . . I gave my kids those "child-centered homemade learning manipulatives" instead of Game Boys, but heck if they began to "spot their own errors, self-assess and complete tasks on their own, and instigate spontaneous math lessons." Dr. Montessori wouldn't last four minutes with my kids.

Maybe we are entirely too precious, raising tiny narcissists who cannot function without their feet sprayed and chakras rearranged. Everything is so earnest that sometimes I think I will just die.

Is it possible to bend the universe too sharply toward our

kids? I think yes. Any child who expects every authority figure and system to be geared toward his happiness is in for a shock. You know what school is for? Learning. You know what else? Sometimes kids get a mean teacher or a class they don't like or an inflexible deadline even though that child was "exhausted the night before." We should not cushion every blow. This is life. Learning to deal with struggle and to develop responsibility is crucial. A good parent prepares the child for the path, not the path for the child. We can still demonstrate gentle and attached parenting without raising children who melt on a warm day.

How can teachers teach when parents demand exceptions and cry foul every time their kid gets crossways? Sometimes we step in and advocate, but sometimes our kids are lame and need to own up. Let them feel the sting of detention, a zero, a lost privilege, a time-out. Let failure instruct them. Otherwise we neuter the teacher's authority and rob our children of responsibility.

And teachers? We'd love to just be parents at home. I absolutely acknowledge the unreasonable demands put upon you (I used to be a teacher), but in the few hours a day we have with our children, we don't want to be tutors, homework drill sergeants, project managers, and trauma counselors. We just want to be moms. Our children are in school seven hours a day, which is enough for a kid. It's almost a full-time job. They should not endure another two hours of homework, especially assignments that are basically Parent Homework (don't get me started).

Can't we all simmer down a bit? Let the teachers teach, the parents parent, and the kids do the learning. Our children will be fine, just as we were. They will figure it out, just as we did.

They don't need every advantage skewed their way and every discomfort fluffed with pillows. I bet they don't even need sandwich dolphins. I am a product of bologna, red Kool-Aid, and home perms, and I turned out okay.

Do we shield our children from harm? Of course. Do we intervene against injustice? Naturally. Do we nurture and adore them? Obviously. But we should also let them fail, wobble, persevere, overcome. Let's not engineer our entire lives around their entertainment and manufactured success. If our kids only expect blessings and exemptions, they will be terrible grown-ups. These are not the adults we want to launch, nor are they the Snowflakes we want our kids to marry. We cannot be the mothers-in-law for these people, oh my gosh. If grown-ups expect sandwich dolphins from their spouses, bosses, churches, friends, and children, this will all be a disaster.

It might be helpful to unpack the root motivations behind our hovering tendencies. I suspect fear is the culprit. Will our kids get left behind? Will they have what everyone else has? Will they come out on top (and by proxy, will we)? Will they get hurt? What if they are just . . . *average*?! We doubt the results of health and maturity, the basic tools that have always produced amazing young adults: hard work, failure, simplicity, gratefulness, restraint, and discipline. We forget that no is an acceptable answer to our kids in a world of the unbridled yes.

We very much underestimate their resilience, and I worry we consider "success" to be a product of the parent's diligence more than the child's. This offers short-term success but sets them up for long-term failure. A kid prepared to work hard, to pay her dues, to own up to her mistakes, and to value instruction is probably going further than the kid who had every advantage skewed her direction and every blow cushioned. Could we identify the lies fear tells us and do the courageous work of parenting against the grain?

So I guess that starts now, right? Kiddies, make your own lunches, do your own laundry, buy your own replacement ID after you left yours on the bus. Write your teacher an apology for doing the worm across her classroom, even though Dad and I laughed our heads off. You want more clothes than we bought? Save your money. Make your own case to the teacher for a higher score. Relinquish your phone for running that mouth. Endure that class. Work for that grade. Try harder next time. Take your licks and learn from them. Put your plate in the dishwasher, for the love of Palmolive.

Better for them to learn these lessons now while the consequences are small than later when they are catastrophic. We are not just raising boys and girls; we are shaping future mamas and daddies and professionals and disciples. It is noble, important work with mega-outcomes. We want our future sons- and daughters-in-law to thank us, not require marriage counseling for their spouses' Codependent Mommy Issues. (Dear Lord, keep my name out of the therapist's office.)

So maybe we lower the bumpers on the bowling lane and see what happens. I bet our kiddos are sturdier than we think. Maybe they don't need every gadget and advantage. Maybe kids grow like all humans do: through struggle, failure, and perseverance. They might have a gear we didn't know about and don't need to be coddled like fragile hothouse plants that can't adapt to new environments. I bet the kids will surprise us.

And if it turns into a shambles? I will personally send you a lifetime supply of sandwich dolphins.

Dear Kids

It is just a random Tuesday, so today is as good as any to tell you all my dreams for your life. I don't want to wait until your gradu- ation parties or rehearsal dinners or some big moment when important words will get swept away in the hustle. Plus, a bunch of this can't wait until you're grown because it matters right now. Also, you are all asleep, so I'm feeling very tender toward you because you are 1.) safe and snug in your beds and 2.) silent. (I love you so, but this family has a lot of words.)

You're just kids, so you have no concept of how much Dad and I think about you. We just seem like bossy parents, I'm sure. One day you'll understand. When you are moms and dads, you'll see. We would forfeit any of our own dreams to make yours hap- pen, but that's hard for you to grasp; we mostly seem like lame buzzkills right now. You'll go crazy mad for your own kids one day and get it.

You span fourth through twelfth grades, so this is our last

year under one roof—the Family Years. I cannot believe it. These childhood years are all you know, but Dad and I realize how special they are, how far they reach, how long you'll talk about them. We will remember these Family Years in similar ways, just from the other side. We know they are fleeting because we've already been through them once at your age. Family Years go fast but they matter for a lifetime.

With Gavin departing soon, then the rest of you launching every other year, our days of influence are shrinking. I guess I want to put pen to paper here, make sure you know exactly what we hope for you and from you. They might not be what you think. Oh sure, we harped on grades all these years, but the honor roll isn't really our main jam. We have dreams other than raising by-the-book kids (not that you ever were).

Kindness. This pulls right to the front. Dad and I have lived half our lives or so, and we've known every type of person. The ones that shine outstanding in our memories are the kind ones. We so deeply want you to be tender toward people. Empathizing is key to a wholehearted life. I pray for your kindness more than your success, because the latter without the former is a tragedy. God measures our entire existence by only two things: how we love Him and how we love people. If you get this right, you can get a million other things wrong.

And guess what? You have the best place to practice right now: public school. I can't remember more insecure, difficult years than middle and high school. You are all a mess, but some kids have it worse, because they are so, so different—and the teen years are not safe for the different. Some of your classmates barely get out the door every day. You see them. They are picked on or mocked or completely ignored, as if they don't even matter. They pretend they don't care or can't hear, but you know they do. These years will hurt for so long.

First, I hope you see them. This is harder than it sounds; you have to learn to see hurt people, because they figure out how to act invisible. Kindness needs recipients. The whole world is filled with lonely and left-out and humiliated and sad kids, and seeing them is the first step. Because they are just as precious as you. If you can learn this during the Family Years, it will change your life, because you'll develop eyes for pain, which is exactly how Jesus walked around on this earth. If your mercy radar is strong now, God can do anything with you later.

My dream is that you see hurting kids and do the simple, brave work of kindness. This isn't fancy at all. It sounds like: *Do you want to sit with us?* or *I really like your outfit* or *What's up, man?* or *What are you reading?* It doesn't seem like much, maybe, but if it's the only kind word they've heard all day, it can literally give them strength to go on.

Sometimes kindness requires more serious courage, because hurt kids make easy targets, and cowards both bully and look the other way. I hope you stand between abusers and the abused, refusing to silently watch one kid break another down. I hope you say NO. I hope you say LEAVE HIM ALONE. I hope you tuck hurt kids into your arms, into your friend circles, protecting them, valuing them. Bring them home to our table, and we will love them together. The tiniest scrap of hope is enough to save a lonely kid from drowning. You'd be surprised how powerful kindness actually is. I am not being dramatic: you can save hearts and lives with grace. Do this good work now, and you will do it for a lifetime.

My next dream for you is the courage to be exactly who you are. Dad and I think you are five dazzling kids. We love and like you. Not one of you is the same as the next, and we wouldn't change a thing. Not one thing. We love your humor and quirks and passion and fire, and it is clear God designed you exactly so. We are tickled to death over you, delighted we get to parent such interesting kids. Seriously. We are smitten with you.

We are in our forties, so we've learned the advantages of being true to ourselves, but you are young when "being yourself" is a slippery concept. It is so tempting to bend, to go along, to fake it. I know this. I remember. I always hated big crowds and loud parties, but I pretended to enjoy both. I wanted to be liked more than I wanted to be genuine. I wish I could go back and tell myself that it wouldn't even matter, that my real friends liked the real me and they were the only ones who would stick.

At your age, it takes courage to march to your own drumbeat. So few kids try. Popularity is a terrible goal, because you have to lose yourself to find it. If you sacrificed one precious part of yourselves, it would be a calamity. At no point, in no environment, among no friends must you be anything but exactly who you are. There is never a need to act less weird or more enthusiastic or extra eager or remotely mean to please someone else. When you want to say no, say no. When you want to say yes, say yes, even if no one else does. Dad and I have your back.

Gavin, you are so freaking funny. You love humor like I do;

listening to stand-up comedy podcasts with you is my favorite thing. Be that guy. Don't diminish your personality; you are wired this way and we can't get enough of it. You are so fun. Sydney, you resemble a grandmotherly librarian who loves the world, recycling, and local food sourcing. You are a joy. If you forfeited one solitary quality, I would die. We are so into you. Caleb, you are this stylish, hysterical kid with big feelings and clear dreams. You know what you love and can't stand injustice, and Dad busts me all the time staring at you with Lovesick Mom Eyes. Ben, you are one of the kindest, brightest kids on earth. You work hard and love hard and have overcome so much to still be so tender. What a delight you are. I cannot believe I get to be your mom. Remy, you are a bright, shining star. You are so loyal and precious, so loving and funny. Girl, no one loves numbers and calendars and dates like you. We wouldn't wish one single thing about you to be different. You are our treasure.

If you learn to be true in childhood, you will bypass the devastating "undoing" so many endure later. You won't have to reinvent, reimagine, or rediscover who you are in your twenties, when you are making the most important decisions of your life (a terrible time for an identity crisis). It will take courage to live truthfully, but do the hard work now or later when it is harder. Some folks never do this and live halfheartedly their entire lives.

Be you, because you are superb.

Finally, let's talk about God. You are a pastor's kids. Sorry about that. We try not to put unreasonable "shoulds" and "should nots" on you guys, but I'm sure we do (you can sort this out with your therapists one day). It's weird for you to think of Dad and me as real people, but we are. We became parents at twenty-three and twenty-five, barely old enough to vote. I know we don't get even half this parenting thing right, but we so hope that however imperfectly we do it, we give you God.

He is the only thing I'm sure of. I have no idea what your careers will be (something that helps you move out) or whom you will marry (please pick fun and funny spouses). I don't know where you will live (Austin) or how many kids you'll have (grandbabes!), but if you love Jesus, I am not afraid for you. Long before you were ours, you were God's. I cannot imagine the plans He has for you, but I'm sure they are spectacular, because He is and you are.

Love God and follow Him. Really, nothing else matters. If you are ever unsure what to do, remember how Jesus loved people. He was the best at it. You can trust Him because anywhere He asks you to go, He has been there too. This is not an easy path, Lovies. Jesus went to hard places and did hard things; He loved folks everyone else hated or despised. But if you trust us at all, believe me: this is the life you want, this Jesus life.

When people fail you—and they will—Jesus is ever faithful. When circumstances tank—and they will—Jesus will hold you fast. He is the most trustworthy, dependable Savior, and you will never be alone. This gives me such comfort, because as imperfect parents who failed often, we are terrified to send you out knowing we didn't do enough. But Jesus is enough for all of us. He is enough for you. No one is safer. No one loves you more. No one will lead you better.

So those are my dreams for you:

Be kind.

Be you.

Love Jesus.

That's about it. Everything else will fall into place. If you are kind and genuine Jesus-lovers, you will marry well, parent well, live well, love well. We are so excited to watch. We believe in you. God gave us five remarkable kids, and these raising-you years are a joy and a gift and the delight of my life.

The launching season begins next year, and I can hardly speak of it. It went so fast. People told me it would and I didn't believe them, but here we are in the home stretch; the finish line is near. The Family Years are waning and it literally takes my breath. (Dad says you are just growing up, not dying, but I'll cry about it IF I WANT TO.) You are my heart's full joy, and if I could write my perfect story from scratch, it would be our exact life. You are my treasures on this earth—mine, so adored. When I am eighty-nine years old, I will look back on the Family Years and say, "We had such a good time."

Be kind, be you, and love Jesus. Dad and I are cheering you on, Beloveds.

CHAPTER 12

Marriage: Have
Fun and Stuff

Brandon and I have been married twenty years. This is shocking because I look so young (please play along), but the explanation for your confusion is that I wed at nineteen. As in, a *teenager* who could not even drink at her own wedding. I have a sixteen-year-old son, and if he announced an engagement in three years, I would lock him in the attic and tell his fiancée he fled to Croatia to find himself and we are very sorry about this unfortunate turn of events but she should just *move it along, sister.* Ridiculous.

However, having weathered the poverty-poor-government-cheese early years, the baby/toddler/preschooler fuzzy years, the "I want to be a writer and no it does not pay" insanity years, and now the one-in-elementary-two-in-middle-two-in-high-school years, we made it. We have five whole children. I've been married longer than I haven't. I've made out with the same man since

AT&T released the first "video telephone" for $1,499.00. (Just four years later I got my first e-mail address and ridiculed, "Oh, right. Like people are going to have home computers to 'e-mail' each other. We aren't millionaires! And what, you're going to write me a note? To my 'e-mail address'? So dumb." No one ever accused me of being a visionary.)

Twenty years in, I've learned a few things. Mostly the hard way. Sure, I planned on being a Darling Lamb Wife, but I accidentally got a fiery personality and forgot to be darling. Plus, I married a man with strong opinions about every solitary thing in the entire universe, past and present. *Gentle* is not an adjective ever wasted on us. We learned our lessons in the trenches of compromise. All due respect to the Resurrection, but two-becoming-one might be the greatest miracle ever.

I'll share our hard-won insights in case you are a Darling Lamb Wife who needn't learn everything the hard way, bless your dear, beloved heart.

1. You are not good at the same things and this is okay.

Brandon and I say that together we make one whole person. In the marriage rhythm, figure out your notes and play them well. This is your part of the song. Stop being mad that your guy is terrible at your notes. Those are yours. He has his. Sure, there is overlap, but you didn't marry your clone. Be happy that you make one whole person together. Brandon will continue to buy me thoughtful, sentimental, exactly-right gifts, and I will continue to mean well. I will care deeply about organic, responsibly-sourced homemade meals, and Brandon will keep taking them to McDonald's when I am traveling. Be good at your half and let your husband be good at his.

2. I'm all for honesty, but pretending has its place.

This might be shocking, but you won't be into all the same things. I mean, sure, perhaps *you* care deeply about the 307-cubic-inch, 200-horsepower V-8 in that 1971 Chevelle SS your husband wants to talk about, but I have to arrange my face into Interested Listening Mode while my mind thinks about William and Kate's baby. Similarly, Brandon says my favorite dancers on *So You Think You Can Dance* are "extremely talented." Bless him, I cannot imagine anything he cares about less, but there he is, doling out compliments. (He benefits from my romantic-dance-watching feelings, so don't throw him a party.) Caring about what your spouse cares about is a big, big deal. Sometimes the Venn diagram crosses perfectly and you actually both love March Madness, and sometimes you do Interested Listening Mode and fake it, because you may not love deer season but you love your man.

3. I'm all for pretending, but honesty has its place.

Politely attending to your hubby's interests is one thing, but withholding crucial honesty is another. I am emotionally guarded, and Brandon's every feeling is in constant plain sight. I internalize and he externalizes. A few years ago, I nursed some hidden resentments in silence, but they came out sideways as these things always do. That entire year was marked by icy silences, cold interactions, and damaging inner monologues. If that doesn't sound like "real marriage troubles," it was relationally catastrophic. We were in the car when Brandon finally broke, saying, "I have no idea what is wrong, but this cannot go on. I can't live like this." I was fighting a battle he didn't know existed, which is spectacularly unfair. My resentment built a stone wall, but voicing it began crumbling the divide. Unattended hurt, anger, and bitterness can destroy even the best marriage. Lean honestly into every hard place, each tender spot, because truthfulness hurts for a minute but silence is the kill shot.

4. Find best couple friends.

I don't care how many couples y'all have to date; keep trying until you find one where $2 + 2 = 4$, or even better, $2 + 2 + 2 = 6$ (this equation could be even larger, but I fear the math would get tedious). We took our first couples' trip ten years ago, and I told Brandon, "Babe, I love you and traveling together is amazing. But not as amazing as traveling with our friends. No offense." Couple relationships are so vital, I literally cannot imagine our adult life without them. I don't mean polite social interaction between slightly coerced adults; I mean friends who come over in nasty pajama pants and openly mock you to your face. The ones who send group texts with dumb videos and create buckets of inside jokes and memories. Where the girls can be with the girls or the guys can be with the guys or the bunch of you go to Cancun for anniversaries. These friendships keep us healthy, grounded, and connected like nothing else does. Like the sage philosophers of White Lion declared, "You're All I Need." And I would add, "Plus our friends. No offense."

5. Lighten up.

One time Brandon and I were playing Scrabble with our friends, and he made me so mad, I swept every tile onto the floor like some lunatic. I destroyed the whole game. (Cackling as I type that. What a freak. To be fair, one of our biggest fights was when I told Brandon to "turn right after the tower," meaning, "the only turn available on the left 'just past that tower' that I am pointing to the left with my pointing arm since a wheat field is on the right," and after missing the turn, he got so mad at me for saying "right" instead of "left" that we didn't speak for a whole day.) Young marrieds, take my advice: Go ahead and lighten up. Don't wait for a Turn Right Here to the Left Meltdown to figure this out. So few issues are actually worth the argument. Marriage is no place to be inordinately sensitive. We cannot prickle over every little thing. Learn to hold the biting remark, the wounded reaction, the irritated retort. Married tongues should be shredded with the amount of ugly words bitten back. Everything cannot be a big deal, because when the big deals actually happen, we're too worn-out to handle them. Who really cares if he always leaves the cabinet doors open? Okay, fine. I do. Whatever, man.

6. Be nice.

We should treat our husbands at least as nicely as we treat the crossing guard. If I wouldn't snap rudely at my girlfriends, I probably shouldn't save my worst behavior for the man I sleep with. Twenty years in, I'm amazed how far basic niceties go. We are past theatrical gestures and emotional torrents; we now settle in nicely between "Here, I poured you some coffee" and "You look pretty today." In our first five years, the magic involved dramatic makeup sex. You know what's sexy at twenty years? Niceness. Compliments after all this time. Thank yous. Apologies. I am over all the drama; give me kindness any old day. Treating your husband like a good friend will preserve your marriage forever. Just act like someone you would want to live with instead of a difficult frenemy.

7. Stick together spiritually.

This is not exact because we are individuals bound in a unit, but walk your spiritual road together. Nothing feels lonelier than one partner a mile behind the other. Ask questions together, discuss what you're learning, struggle together, take the same classes, do the same studies, refuse to leave the other in the dust. Serving together revolutionized our marriage. If one is ahead, prioritize patience and nag-resistance. God isn't a wedge between spouses; if you aren't walking side by side, I believe God will wait for you both. Press Pause. Don't give the spiritual depth to your church or friends and leave housekeeping leftovers for your man. Grow together, learn together, seek together, serve together. This is the most eternal portion of your union; treat it with utmost care.

8. Stop trying to change each other.

Listen, young marrieds, I want to save you some grief: Your husband is who he is. His temperament and tendencies are basically set. If he is a serial planner, stop forcing spontaneity onto him. If he is a Fun Time Guy, quit wishing he were a squared-away engineer. For the most part, you got what you married; and the sooner you accept the man who walked down that aisle, the better. Waste no energy trying to fundamentally change him. This will leave you bitter and won't work anyway. Hear me: Every single person has a downside, including you. The grass is not greener anywhere. Every marriage includes two sinful, aggravating human beings. Grace is our only hope. Accept him—the best parts, the medium parts, and the scourge-y parts (you have them as well). When a partner clearly doesn't like *who you are*, it is so defeating. If you are trying to change the very way your husband is wired, take the nooses off both your necks. Set him free, and you may remember how much you like the rest of him.

9. Have fun.

Sometimes you have to break out the running man when a Vanilla Ice song plays. Every husband should occasionally be splashed by his wife's impulsive cannonball. I say the couple that embarrasses their children together has a 100 percent chance of making it. Brandon and I regularly sit in middle school programs and make fun of kids. (Don't scold us. Middle schoolers are awesomely awkward. Including ours.) Laughing together is the best marriage offers, in my opinion. Fun is so underrated. Fun is powerful glue. Fun helps us like each other, not just love each other. Life will deliver plenty of struggles; we need not manufacture grown-up, sober moments. We'll get those in spades. Let us inject marriage with silliness and laughter and funny board games and dumb movies and ridiculous dance moves at a cousin's wedding. Catch your husband's eye across the room as he tells a funny story and let him know with your face: *I like you, man. You are telling that story like a boss.*

10. Have lots of sex.

This is just really, sincerely a thing. Whether the guy way (make love *to* feel loved) or the girl way (make love *because* you feel loved), at the end of twelve minutes, you're both happy. (Young marrieds, those all-afternoon sexy Sundays are doomed. If Brandon wanted sex for three hours now, I would relocate to Canada. That doesn't sound like a treat; it sounds like a UTI. Just keep it normal, man.) Sex is magic. It brings us together and keeps us together. I cannot possibly address all potential sexual baggage here, but I'll say this: Anything worth fighting for is worth fighting through, and healthy sex in your marriage is one. Sex can be so much more than concession. If your husband knows you love and want him, you empower him in every other area. This is one place he is vulnerable, and your desire in the bedroom is more than loving; it is powerful. If you have no idea where to start, if marital troubles are overwhelming and you can't discern next steps, begin with sex and see what miracles can happen.

૭ல

Marriage is crazy work, but it is good work. Two people must regularly get over themselves and fight for love. There is no coasting; it's pretty much foot on the gas forever. Some parts get easier and others get harder. Marriage is completely beautiful and sometimes not so much, and many of us will fight our way back from disintegration to create something stronger than before—with scars, of course.

Thousands of times during a life built together, you walk up to a moment and choose: I choose your happiness, your health, your well-being. I choose to build you up rather than strip away. I choose you over the Fake Shiny Other who promises something better. I choose forgiveness because otherwise we are hopeless. I choose to believe in you. I choose this life we've built, these kids we've created, this legacy we're forming. I choose God in you and me, making us more like His Son, writing a lovely story with our life together. I choose you and I would choose you all over again. As Jane Eyre said of her Mr. Rochester, "I know what it is to live entirely for and with what I love best on earth. I hold myself supremely blessed—blessed beyond what language can express; because I am my husband's life as fully as he is mine."[1]

CHAPTER 13

Jesus Kids

Good reader, I was exactly the Church Youth Group Girl you think I was. Christian T-shirts and youth choir with a side of sanctimony. It pains me to admit this, but my class voted me "Most Inspirational" my senior year. I was a lot of fun, bless my heart.

I grew up immersed in typical Christian culture: heavy emphasis on morality, fairly dogmatic, linear, and authoritative. Because my experience was so homogenous and my skill set included Flying Right, I found wild success within the paradigm. My interpretations were rarely challenged by diversity, suffering, or disparity. Since the bull's-eye was good behavior (we called it "holiness"), I earned an A.

But as I careened into adulthood, my firm foundation endured some havoc. I noticed very few of my Third Day Acquire the Fire Disciple Now Weekend Mercy Me compatriots sticking with church after high school, all of whom had been "on fire" just a few short years before. Because I chose a small Baptist college, my youth group environment was preserved in a collegiate setting, and I remained confused and slightly betrayed by the mass exodus of my friends. My own spiritual tension was delayed and I didn't understand the migration until later.

Here is where this gets real for us mamas: this is absolutely the trend. Ranier Research found that nearly three-quarters of American youths leave church between ages eighteen and twenty-two, while the Barna Group estimates that by age twenty-nine, 80 percent of the churched population will become "disengaged" with church culture.[1]

That's 80 percent. Gone.

These are our kids.

A recent nationwide poll on religious identification noted that respondents with "no religion" (The Nones) constituted the only group that grew in every state. According to Drew Dyck, reporting for *Christianity Today*, "a whopping 22 percent of 18- to 29-year-olds claimed no religion, up from 11 percent in 1990. The study also found that 73 percent of Nones came from religious homes; 66 percent were described by the study as 'de-converts.'"[2]

The mechanism is not holding. Religion is leaving young adults disinterested at best, hostile at worst. It must be failing to capture their loyalty because these numbers don't lie. A quick investigation reveals common objections to church:

- Its emphasis on morality and voting records over matters like justice and transformation
- A me-and-mine stance against you-and-yours

- A defensive posture, treating unchurched or dechurched people like adversaries
- An opposition to science
- Its consumerism
- Its group hostility toward the gay community
- An arrogance rather than humility

Our second graders might not navigate this tension yet, but their seminal moment is right around the corner. Better to regard the dominant trend than assume our kids will be in the satisfied (but shrinking) 20 percent. What can we do? How do we raise our kids to love Jesus long after we stop taking them to Sunday school?

The bad news is there is no system, no ten-step program to ensure success. Kids are their own people; this is a clear downside of children. Parents of littles think they are still in control of outcomes, but mamas of bigs know better. Kids are actual humans with hearts, minds, ideas, and laundry lists of sins to handle. There is no secret way around their humanity.

We can put up good markers but cannot chart their courses.

Let me pause to acknowledge the fear button I maybe just pushed. The last thing I want to do is terrify my beloved readers, but we can't work through what we don't acknowledge. (I would rather us absorb these sobering statistics now than suffer shock and dismay later, stunned by our kids' spiritual struggles.) As we move forward in this discussion, remember this: God intensely loves our kids. He is always working for them, toward them. No matter how far off the beaten path they may or may not go, He'll never leave them. Parenting is as much about our sanctification as theirs; it teaches us to trust God and listen humbly, to commit our greatest treasures to His safekeeping. No one wants more for our kids than God (or even knows what that "more" looks like), and He is a mighty leader. We can confidently give Him our fear, our hopes, and our kids.

As parents, we are only marker-makers—it is the best we can do—so I have some ideas for markers. First, pay attention to the grievances listed above. This is no time to defend our perspectives and dig in our heels. We have to raise the kids we have, not the kids we were. Young adults are abandoning church, so we can either listen carefully or watch their backs as they go. We cannot be more committed to our methods than our message. Do we want to raise disciples? Then pay equal attention to what isn't working as much as what is.

Treat their questions and concerns with respect, because in my opinion, they have a decent pulse on cultural Christianity. Rather than starting with, "You are young and clueless," maybe we say, "Tell me what you see and what concerns you. What draws you to church? What pushes you away? What do your friends say?" Humility attracts the next generation as easily as arrogance alienates them. This is so crucial. If we dismiss this conversation, we dismiss them from the church.

Deeper still, we examine the spiritual temperature of our homes. Are we arrogant and judgmental? Do we subtly (or overtly) teach our children to suspect anyone "other"? Do we put mainly defensive spiritual tools in our kids' hands, fostering an "against them" rather than "for them" posture? Do we emphasize behavior over character? Because good behavior won't guarantee anything. If they don't love Jesus and people, it matters zero if they remain virgins and don't say the F-word. We must shepherd their hearts, not just their hemlines.

Jesus operates beyond the tidy boundaries of good behavior. Rather than simply enforce His rules, we should show our kids His kingdom. That's where they'll discover a Savior to fall in love with. Out where life is messy and relationships are complicated. Where the poor struggle and grace is a lifeline. If we want to raise disciples, we'd better take them to where Jesus is working, because they'll discover His appeal more quickly in the field than in sanitized church classrooms or on behavior charts.

The next generation is screaming, "We can't find God in church! How does God work in the broken places? Why are Christians so mean and scared and defensive? Where is the 'good news' part? Why does the church spend so much money on itself? Why do believers insist on Jesus being in the White House when He spent His time with lepers? If He didn't redeem the world on the throne, then why would He do it now? Why does so much Christianity smack of power and aggression when Jesus was humble and subversive?"

These are good questions that deserve consideration.

We are raising postmodern kids in a postmodern generation. An incredibly reduced explanation of modern thought (which most of us have at least one foot in) would be: *I have all the answers and so can you.* This drove society for three hundred years. The shift to postmodernism began in our childhoods and absolutely defines the next generation. Their mantra is: "I don't have all the answers and neither do you." Opposite Day. No wonder we are experiencing a major failure to connect.

What many of us embraced as solid and certain seems condescending and exclusive to them. Values that felt trustworthy to some of us—authority, tradition, reason, logic, absolute truth—read like easily dismantled propaganda to postmoderns. Authority—parents, church leaders, government—has failed the next generation in profound ways. Postmoderns will not swallow ideology just because someone said it tastes good. Cynicism is often their obstacle, but also it protects their hearts from further betrayal. They can sniff a sham a mile away.

Postmoderns experience God differently than most of us did at their age. I learned apologetics and practiced defending my faith (*I have all the answers and so can you*). They hunger for community and justice, humility and anticonsumerism. They don't like slick. They don't trust a leader without a limp. Since they question everything, they require safe spiritual environments where struggles are welcomed and discussed (*I don't have all the answers and neither do you*). They must be allowed to wrestle without being shamed, or they'll default to their open-armed peers and we will lose them.

We cannot shrug this off because this is the next generation of the church. If we drop the baton here, sociologists predict a fully post-Christian culture within two generations. Our kids need spiritual mentors, and if a new language and posture will lead them, then we better hit our knees, pray for humility, and beg God to help us raise disciples that love Him beyond our homes. We prioritize transformation over methodology, because our rules have a shelf life but loyalty to Jesus does not. Let's keep the baby and change the bathwater.

Postmoderns share several key values with the gospel, and in these places, Jesus makes sense and the church feels relevant. These biblical touch points fuse the generational divide. Care of the poor and outcast, for starters. This makes sense to our kids. And to Jesus! Bonus! Same page! Mama, love outliers in the name of Jesus and your children will notice. Make this a family priority. Teach them: *This is how we love, this is where we spend our dollars, this is how we serve our city.* This deeply matters to our kids now, certainly into adolescence, and urgently into young adulthood. If the idea of Jesus gets muddy in the sanctuary, Jesus becomes clear again in the margins. Give Sanctuary Jesus something to stick to in the real world and the Bible will feel true once more.

Protecting open, nonjudgmental dialogue with our kids is key. Start young, because when they are sixteen, they may feel as though they need permission to ask hard spiritual questions without getting shut down, patronized, or dismissed. Fear makes parents react dogmatically (Slippery slope! Dangerous questions! Future heretic!), but God never turns away a seeker and neither should we. Our children can press extremely hard on the gospel and it will hold.

We must waive the lecture and embrace listening. What are they actually saying? What is confusing to them? What do they think? Where is the rub? Let's hear them, then engage them. So many students seek our counsel with the same opener: "I can't talk to my parents." Surely we'd rather discuss our kids' doubts than lose our voices altogether. I want mine to know they are safe across the table no matter what comes out of their mouths. I prefer their honesty and proximity over silence and detachment. Kids want to be mentored, not ruled.

Finally, let's give them substance. When young adults between ages eighteen and thirty-five were polled nationwide and asked, "What would draw you or keep you at a church?" they listed the following four tenets: 1.) community, 2.) social justice, 3.) *depth*, and 4.) mentorship.[3] A youth group culture geared toward entertainment is not working. Face it: We cannot out-entertain the world. If discipleship programs hinge on amusement, they'll come now but won't stay later. Why would they?

Believe it or not, kids crave depth. They want to grapple with theology. They are malnourished from too much spiritual soda pop, and they want wine. By attempting to attract them with cultural relevance, the church accidentally became irrelevant— like when parents try to be cool. Turns out they don't want their parents to be cool. They just want them to be parents who don't woo their loyalty and coddle their feelings. Real parents say, "Get out of bed and do your chores." Because they are preparing their kids *to grow up one day.*

Let's give them the goods. Let's put the hard stuff in front of them. We shouldn't patronize their intelligence because kids are absolutely capable of spiritual depth. Let's teach them to serve and care about the world beyond their Xboxes. And we have to lead with our lives, not just our lips, because kids can smell a fake. Our sincerity is so crucial, we shouldn't lead like this if we are unwilling to go first. Better to be entirely apathetic than blatantly hypocritical. They can overcome the first before the second. As long as we lead by example, we can make epic screw-ups and live to tell.

Remember this: No matter what, our children belong to God and He is very much paying attention. He is always at work; we are but one piece of their story. Our kids may detour. So many will crash and burn. They could walk away and they could come back. They will ultimately make their own spiritual decisions, and no formula ensures any outcome. We cannot guarantee their safety or loyalty, their path or decisions. The best parents can have children who self-destruct, and the worst parents can have kids who thrive.

The best we can do is give them Jesus. Not rules, not behaviors, not entertainment, not shame. I have no confidence in myself but every confidence in Jesus. He is such a relief, isn't He? He is always the true answer, the strongest touchstone, the best example. When I am grasping as a spiritual mentor to my kids, there He is. When words and ideas and "right answers" fail me, His life and legacy deliver. With good reason my kids may doubt their parents, church, Christian culture, and their own understanding, but it is harder to doubt a Savior as good as Jesus. He is so incredibly dependable.

Jesus is the only thing that will endure. He trumps parenting techniques, church culture, tight boundaries, and best-laid plans. Jesus can lead our children long after they've left our homes. He will lead them when our work is through.

So let's give our kids Jesus and trust Him to lead, even if we don't see results for five years, ten years, or until the other side of this life. Because no matter what their spiritual futures contain—the new trends, new kind of church, new worldview, new systems—Jesus will remain. He is the only constant, the only Savior that held through the ages.

Jesus is the best marker that exists, so let's raise Him high.

CHAPTER 14

Thank-You Notes (Part 2)

Thank you, Shoppers Without Children. I know my toddler should not be standing in the cart/eating the cookies before I buy them/climbing to the top shelf /asking other shoppers why they are "so fat." I didn't actually coach my kindergartner to announce loudly in Aisle 9, "You loved me since you first saw my head pop out of you, right, Mommy?" I wasn't aware you were the grocery police, but thank you for your unsolicited advice, criticism, and outright shaming techniques. How nice for you that "your children never behaved like this." Sincerely, A Mom on the Edge.

Thank you, Pre-Mixed Mango Margaritas, for helping me get through middle school again as a thirty-eight-year-old mom. It's the only way. If you have any other friends, send them.

Thank you, No Cell Phone Rule on Planes. You have saved the lives of the people around me, or at least prevented some serious passive-aggressive sighing and side eye on my part. Should the airlines ever override this rule, start listening for the Four Horsemen of the apocalypse, because surely this would indicate the end times. Sincerely, Introverted Frequent Flyer Who Wears Headphones with No Music so as Not to Be Spoken To.

Thank you, *Angry Birds*, for helping justify screen time for my kids. I'm now positive they will ace physics someday. (I'm also counting on *Minecraft* for engineering, *Madden NFL* for strategy skills, and Disney Princess apps for reverse self-esteem. Be the classroom we are pretending you are, Handhelds.)

Thank you, Ponchos, for making it acceptable to wear a blanket around in public and call it style. I'd like to also thank your little partner, Leggings, for helping me be cute and comfy in my poncho without any annoying chub-rub on my upper thighs. You make comfortable "fashion" possible whilst going for thirds in the buffet line. (I'd also like to thank Autocorrect for turning *jeggings* into *jogging*, reminding me that if I did jog, I might be able to button actual jeans.)

Thank you, Facebook, for being the ultimate proof that being popular in high school means nothing as an adult.

Thank you, E-reader, for your highly reflective surface into which I can look downward and see my face's future once my skin has lost all its remaining elasticity. I want a digital screen, not a terrifying mirror. Please work on this in your labs. Signed, Lady Whose Hanging Face Keeps Scaring Her As She Reads *Gone Girl*.

Thank you, School Pickup Line, for showing me the under-belly of School Moms. Only in your line can I be flipped off and cut off by the same women I am forced to pair up with at class parties and field trips. This is not at all awkward, and I look forward to these vehicular aggressions every single day. You are a delight.

Thank you, Beautiful Preteen and Adolescent Daughters, fruit of my loins, for keepin' it real by reminding me daily that, although I've been on this planet for over forty years, I still have a lot to learn. And you're just the two to teach it to me. Thank you for putting up with me while I try to figure life out. Love, Your Poor Little Dumb-Dumb Mom.

Thank you, Treadmill, for being the most expensive clothes hanger ever.

Thank you, Person Having a Cell Phone Conversation in the Public Bathroom Stall Right Next to Me at Target, for the reminder that nothing is sacred (or sanitary) anymore. Not only do I know your digestive habits now, but I also know that your cousin Lucy is marrying a loser the whole family hates and you are "not about to pay $120 on a dress for a lame wedding." Good talk.

Thank you, People Who Ask If I'm Pregnant, even though my youngest child is in third grade. You keep me dialed into scriptures on taming my tongue. Thanks for helping me grow in the Word.

Thank you Eighth-Grade Math, for getting me as close as I've ever been to wearing a straitjacket. I have two graduate degrees, but thanks to "new math," my thirteen-year-old now thinks she is smarter than me. Where is the wine? Sincerely, Parent Who Evidently Cannot Divide.

Thank you, Yoga Pants, for allowing me to look like I just worked out! That I am a healthy and productive person, when really I'm basically wearing pajamas while running errands. My unwashed hair and yesterday's makeup add to the charade, so I'm sure folks wonder why such a workout queen still needs to lose twenty pounds. Whatever, YP. I love you. You are my uniform.

FRIENDS, NEIGHBORS, STRANGERS, AND ENEMIES

CHAPTER 15

Supper Club

After I'd been married one year, I served my father-in-law canned ham.

I clearly haven't always loved food and cooking. I was a young married domestic tragedy. After feeding my new husband's father pressed meat, I graduated to Prego over boiled spaghetti—my fancy dinner, including garlic salt sprinkled on white bread (bless my heart). I regularly bought Hamburger Helper. I put fish sticks on hot dog buns with ketchup. Ladies and gentlemen, I served Veg-All.

It was all a disaster. Then I had babies every other year because no one told me not to, and they wanted to eat every day. I meant to learn cooking, but I was too busy keeping small people alive. This survivor mentality infected the kitchen, so cooking produced nothing but resentment and irritation. I was shocked daily that I had to cook dinner again. *What's for dinner, you ask? Well, I guess I'll just nurse this baby and change all these diapers and wrestle this house from the grip of entropy and play Legos for the ten millionth time and also cook a nourishing meal for everyone EVERY DAY! Hey, honey, after dinner cleanup and the bath and bedtime marathon, let's have meaningful sex! Please grope me more than usual because I haven't been felt up enough today.*

I was a delight.

This is literally how it changed. One year on January 1, I asked myself, "What can I do better this year? I have space for one tiny self-improvement . . ." And the answer was cooking. Since these people insisted on eating *every day*, I needed a solution that didn't include cereal for dinner and a growing stew of bitterness.

So I flipped a switch. I started watching Food Network and reading cookbooks. I made an account on allrecipes.com. I bought exotic, fancy ingredients like garlic. I decided the cooking hour should be pleasant: good music playing, a glass of wine, good company (behaving children are welcomed, fighting children are banished). Then I started gardening and watching food documentaries and giving Big Food Industry the side eye and, oh my gosh, now I have ten chickens. It became a whole thing.

Honestly, I just decided to love food.

So when my friend Jamie sent this e-mail four years ago, I was all ears. Sent to three girls, she wrote: "You guys don't know each other but I know all of you. We would make a great pack of couples. Would you consider starting a Supper Club together? Pretty sure the chemistry will totally work and we all love food." Why would eight strangers agree to a monthly commitment sight unseen?

I can't believe we all said yes.

Here were the rules:

1. One night a month, rotating houses.
2. No kids. (Since we have *sixteen* children between us, SC starts at 8:00 p.m. and the hosts' kids are already in bed or bribed with Cheetos and movies. The other parents get sitters—unless they are awesome like me and Melissa and have big kids to babysit, in which case actual supervision is an incredibly loose concept.)
3. When you host, do everything: plan, shop, cook, and clean. So three out of four months, just show up, drink wine, eat amazing food, laugh until you cry, and leave your friend's kitchen an absolute crime scene.
4. The food is serious. If you haven't started planning your menu a week in advance, you are in the weeds. Don't you dare put taco soup on the table.
5. All anyone can bring to SC is wine. And you'd better bring some or die trying.
6. SC is any night we make it work, which means we've seen 1:00 a.m. on a Tuesday and paid brutally. (After one such late night, we bemoaned our exhaustion in a group text the next day. Brandon wrote: "We made the littles eat breakfast at school this morning. Hope the 'pancake on a stick with sugar syrup' works out.")
7. What happens at SC stays at SC. Failure to comply will result in flogging.

When I recall our first Supper Club, I'm tickled we had to introduce ourselves, because now I know everything that ever happened to these people since the day they were born. I know their middle names, everything about their parents, every nuance of their kids, their music, habits, dreams, most embarrassing moments, failures, secrets, preferences (even if Wolfgang Puck crafted it from the ground-up dust of fairy wings, Brad would not eat dessert), future plans, humor, everything.

Our families vacation together each summer because this turned into something more than dinner, as good things often do. We cheer on each other's published books, CD releases, new babies, completed adoptions, new podcasts, new jobs, sabbaticals. We give each other permission to dream. We give each other permission to rest. We give each other permission to grieve. We have the funniest group texts on planet Earth, and should they ever become public, we will all move to Peru.

And in the middle of it all, we have the food, the table, the bread, the wine.

When I start planning for SC, I think: *These are my precious friends. I want to feed them well.* We will gather around lamb stew or lobster bisque or homemade pasta or beef bourguignon, we will pour peppery cabernet or cold champagne, and we'll dig into life together. Sometimes the menu is ethnic and exotic, sometimes comforting and rich, but it all sets the table for laughter, the best kinds of conversation, tears if we need to shed them, embarrassing stories if we need to tell them.

Some nights we go around the table with a prompt: Would you rather be rich or famous? What is your high and low from this year? Justin Bieber: legit or not? What kind of old person do you want to be? What is your worst holiday memory? Phil Donahue or Sally Jessy Raphael? Other nights one person gets the microphone because there is so much to talk about, so much to process. Some seasons are like that. Good friends can discuss the Bieb or a lost adoption. The table can handle it all.

Lest you think us undiscovered chefs, culinary failures still occur after four years of cooking for each other. The Hatmakers once served overcooked deer steak the consistency of bark, with no possible recovery for the palate. The Navarros served pasta alfredo that kept us in the bathroom for twenty-four hours and put Aaron on the brink of dysentery. There was a canned green beans incident still too raw to discuss.

Other times the food wobbled for good reason. Like the day we were hosting and Melissa's dad went into the hospital, an hour and a half away. This was a no-brainer: we packed up our pots and pans, homemade egg rolls, pad Thai ingredients, and five different sauces into a dozen containers; picked up paper plates along the way; and the six of us drove to Temple and put it all together in her family's home. Loaded up every dirty dish and drove them back to Austin four hours later. Sure, the egg rolls would have fared better without the drive, but our friend wouldn't have. The food is just the preview, the intro, the setup. It gives the real story something to stick to.

When I assess our recent blessings, Supper Club is one of the uppermost. Who knew corn cakes with jalapeño butter could create such community? While our senses were busy enjoying the food, our hearts fell in love before we knew what was happening. Somewhere amid fresh bruschetta, grilled pizza, and buttery Chardonnay, we transformed from people who love food to people who love each other—the best kind of alchemy.

Dear reader, nothing would make me happier than your own SC. Don't underestimate its magic. It's not just food; it's holy ground, sacred space.

I'll even get you started. This meal is so delicious, you will cry tears. There is a whole bunch of chopping required, but surely we can run a knife through some onions. It plates up so beautifully and tastes so good, you will be a star.

$$\mathcal{O}\!\mathcal{J}$$

Delicious Yummy Pretty Pad Thai
Serves 4–6

Let's do this.

First, the sauce and noodles: I buy these ingredients online and they are delivered to my doorstep because this is a good time to be alive in America.

3 T. palm sugar

2 T. tamarind concentrate

2 T. fish sauce

8 oz. rice noodles

In a small pot on low, heat the sugar, tamarind, and fish sauce together until the sugar is dissolved. Then take off heat and set aside. Place the rice noodles in hot water in a bowl and let them soften while you chop.

(A word or two. One, I double this and freeze the extra sauce. Less work next time. Two, *fish sauce does not smell good while cooking and I don't want the drama of it the next time I make this.* I suggest making this sauce when fussy, judgmental children are not around. They will wail and whine and ask you, "What are you feeding us oh my gosh? WHY DO YOU HATE US?" You don't need this nonsense. You work too hard for this.)

Get all your chopping done first, because pad Thai is quick work and these ingredients need to be ready to go. Chop chop.

2 large shallots, chopped

4 garlic cloves, chopped

2 carrots, shredded

1 bunch of cilantro, chopped

3 green onions, sliced into one-inch lengths

4–5 radishes, thinly sliced*

2–3 cups mung bean sprouts**

8 oz. extra-firm tofu, cut into one-inch-long and one-
  fourth-inch-wide matchsticks***

*I love radishes, but if you feel overwhelmed about them, just skip. But honestly? Radishes deserve more love than they get. *They are just radishes.* Slice them on your mandolin and wonder why you thought bad thoughts toward radishes. They are crunchy and delicious. People should stop being hateful toward radishes.

**Mung bean sprouts are difficult to find because of pathogens or some nonsense. If you go to an Asian grocery store, you can find enormous bags for like five cents. The Asians aren't about to stop selling mung bean sprouts because of bacteria, for the love. Americans are so precious with their food. We must drive the Asians crazy. If you can't find or get these, you can skip them— but your pad Thai will be the lesser for it and you're letting the FDA win.

***Fine. I don't put the tofu in my pad Thai. I just don't love it, okay? I already endured drama from the fish sauce and I don't feel like discussing tofu with these people.

Have ready:

10 oz. raw shrimp, peeled and deveined; or, boneless
  chicken sliced in really thin strips
2 eggs, lightly beaten
5 T. vegetable oil
1/2 cup roasted peanuts, chopped
lime, halved (for juice and garnish)

Have all this ready, including your softened and drained rice noodles. Take a picture of it. The piles look nice. The radishes are particularly pretty. Someone should bear witness to your culinary prowess.

Get a big wok. This is important. Pad Thai cannot be made in a little skillet or it will steam and clump together and you will regret it the rest of your life. You also need two wooden spatulas.

Don't bring flimsy utensils to this party. Your spatulas are going to toss and fry all this like a boss.

Get ready because pad Thai is a quick marathon, which in my opinion, is the best kind of marathon—over in minutes. Good Lord, we're not Olympians.

Heat three tablespoons of oil in your wok over medium-high heat. Your wok needs to be really hot, you guys. Add the drained noodles and toss until they are coated in the oil and have become a little more pliable. Practice your two-spatula approach. Look how good you are at it! Get under it, lift, and toss. You want all your ingredients to touch the hot skillet at some point. Do this for about one minute.

Add the sauce and toss noodles until totally coated. (I add hot chili sauce here too, but know thy people and cook accordingly.) Your two spatulas are earning their keep. About one minute here.

Push the noodles to one side of the pan, then add another two tablespoons of oil to the empty side. Sauté the shallots, carrots, garlic, radishes, tofu, and green onions. Toss with your two spatulas constantly for about a minute. Add the chicken or shrimp to the veggies and toss for another two or three minutes until they are cooked through.

You are almost done. You are a hero.

Make a well in the center of the pan. Add the eggs, and scramble with the tip of your spatula. About one minute.

Now toss the whole kit and caboodle together with your spatulas. Remove from heat and fold in half of the mung bean sprouts. Pour the wok's contents onto a big serving platter. Sprinkle with the remaining bean sprouts, chopped cilantro, and chopped roasted peanuts. Squeeze fresh lime juice over the whole thing.

Look at it. It is gorgeous. You made that, and it is restaurant quality. There is a 100 percent chance you will post this to Instagram. It is so good, you cannot believe it. Now that you've done it once, it is a thousand times easier forevermore. Your people will love this. Serve it with chopsticks and they will throw a parade in your honor. WELL DONE, COOKING WARRIOR.

CHAPTER 16

Porches as Altars

If you didn't grow up in a Christian subculture, this will probably make zero sense. But for those of you who did, do you remember Sunday Night Church?

Listen. Any yahoo could manage Sunday Morning Church, but SNC was for the diehards. Having barely snuck in an afternoon nap, it was back to church at 6:00 p.m. for the dyed-in-the-wool Baptists like us. We didn't even play, man.

SNC was the canvas for looser programming, after having pledged allegiance to the choir, the Sandi Patty–esque soloist, and the senior pastor in the a.m., SNC was the space for traveling evangelists, missionary testimonies, Youth Group Camp Reporting Night, and my dad's favorite: quartets. (To this day, I can pick out a bass line in a gospel ensemble in one bar.) It was a whole 'nother deal when the pastor wore his casual khakis and *no tie*. Having taken those liberties, we were one emotional outburst away from clapping.

But I'll tell you why I loved SNC. As you maybe surmised, it wasn't the guest preachers or handbell concerts. In fact, it had nothing to do with programming. It was simply this: My youth group went out every Sunday night after church. We begged five dollars off our parents and put one dollar of gas into willing drivers' cars (true story) and unleashed a gaggle of young evangelicals onto the unsuspecting city of Wichita, Kansas. Mr. Gatti's, sand volleyball, swimming, whatever.

These nights comprise some of my favorite memories.

I don't even know if Sunday Night Church still exists, but we've carried the tradition forward. Our little hippie church doesn't have a night service, but Brandon and I and our two best couple friends gather every weekend for SNC on one of our porches. After the big lunch has digested and naps have been taken and the littles have been put to bed, *it's time.*

After sussing out details, we gather on someone's patio with wine and cheese and leftover desserts, and *we have us some church.* We've solved every problem on Earth or hashed it out real good. Usually SNC is for laughing and pure folly, watching funny YouTube videos like a bunch of juveniles. Sometimes one of us is in the weeds, and we do a lot of listening. Occasionally we wade into theology, as we've all stretched in surprising ways these last few years and like to try our ideas out with each other. Or we watch football and pledge to finally break up with the Cowboys.

The same connective thread remains twenty-plus years after my youth group days: If Jesus is the heart of the church, people are the lifeblood. There is a reason He created community and told us to practice grace and love and camaraderie and presence. People soften the edges and fill in the gaps. Friends make up some of the best parts of the whole story.

We live in a strange, unprecedented time when face-to-face relationships are becoming optional. It's tricky, this new online connectivity, because it can become meaningful and true; it has given way to actual friendships I treasure. But it can also steal from friends on porches, the ones who truly know you, who talk about real life over nachos. Online life is no substitute for practiced, physical presence, and it will never replace someone looking you in the eye, padding around your kitchen in bare feet, making you take a blind taste test on various olives, walking in your front door without knocking.

I meet women all over the country, and I look so many in the eyes and see loneliness. People crave what they have always craved: to be known and loved, to belong somewhere. Community is such a basic human need. It helps us weather virtually every storm. If Jesus' basic marching orders were 1.) to love God and 2.) to love people, then the fruit of that obedience includes being loved by God and loved by people. We give and get here. According to Jesus, the love of God and people is the substance of life.

Isn't it? Nothing can happen—no tragedy, no suffering— that cannot be survived through the love of God and people. This is holy territory: a loyal friend on the other end of the line, a companion on your doorstep holding King Ranch chicken casserole because sometimes that's all there is to do. When you say to me, "I will see you through this," I can endure. Between God's strength and yours, I have enough. We are not promised a pain-free life but are given the tools to survive: God and people.

It is enough.

The church certainly tries to foster community, bless it. We at least know how essential it is. So we organize Life Groups (see also: Restore Groups, Community Groups, Home Groups, Cell Groups, Youth Groups, Women's Groups, or—kickin' it like my Baptists—Sunday school). We try to provide structure for folks to belong, to be known. Sometimes it works like magic and sometimes it *so* doesn't. You can lead a horse to water, but sometimes the horse is awkward and weird, you know? I've had small groups create friends for life and others that felt a teeny bit like sustained torture.

I guess I prefer something a bit more organic, less program-driven. Instead of waiting around for church to assemble a perfect group dynamic of People Who Can Meet on Tuesdays, maybe just invite some folks over. A shared table is the supreme expression of hospitality in every culture on earth. When your worn-out kitchen table hosts good people and good conversation, when it provides a safe place to break bread and share wine, your house becomes a sanctuary, holy as a cathedral. I've left a friend's table as sanctified and renewed as any church service. If you have a porch, then you have an altar to gather around.

Don Miller described a powerful purpose I cannot quit thinking about. He and his wife Betsy decided their home was sacred, and their ambition was to help restore what the world stole that day to every visitor. Isn't that the loveliest thought you've ever heard? They fill their home with friends, travelers, neighbors, and comrades who sign the underside of their table upon leaving, hopefully refreshed, restored in some small way. This doesn't require a therapy license or a culinary degree. Heck, sometimes it only means making meatball subs and being a good listener. What an acute assessment of the power of the table. How profoundly holy. I love it so much I painted "RESTORE" across my entryway, a banner over every precious soul who walks in and out of our home.

Loneliness can be a prison, but we have keys. You needn't wait for someone to open the bars. If you can make a pot of chili and use a cell phone, then you can create community. If you want to wait until your house is perfect and you aren't nervous, then just forget it. This is an imperfect apparatus, thank goodness. It requires people with true faces, courageously being seen. There is no alternative to genuine connection. Sorry. Community has to start somewhere, and that somewhere should be sincere. Otherwise you build a flimsy house of cards. Run the risk analysis and decide if safety is worth the loneliness prison. I suggest it is not.

We have the keys, you guys! They look like tables and couches, beef stew and crusty French bread. They include patio chairs and music, football on the TV and cold beer. They involve a simple e-mail invite for Friday night and burgers on the grill. They say, "Bring your kids and we'll lock them all in the backyard with Popsicles." The keys include good questions and good listening around a fire pit; they certainly contain stories and laughter. They don't require fussing or fluffing, so don't let anything stop you, because a messy kitchen only tells me someone cares enough to feed me, which is a good key.

Instead of waiting for community, provide it, and you'll end up with it anyway.

Maybe just start looking around. Let's not overcomplicate this. Who lives nearby? Who is new to town? Who seems inter-esting or funny or smart or silly? Who is in your stage of life? Who could use a warm bowl of soup and cornbread? Who is lonely? If you're super nervous, invite two friends or two couples over for a buffer to avoid potential awkward grenades. You might enjoy pitch-perfect chemistry and blaze into your second date, but if not, you still provided a safe, warm place for someone to be welcomed. That is good work.

Sometimes these things start a little stiff, so be patient. My best advice is just to show up and be truthful. Be the kind of friend you are hoping for. Trust me, no one wants a perfect friend who can't offer a minute of transparency. We can get that on Pinterest. Our souls ache for real people in real homes with real kids and real lives. We may carefully curate online identities with well-chosen pictures and selective information, but doing so leaves us starving for something true. I seek only friends who bleed and sweat and laugh and cry. Don't fear your humanity; it is your best offering.

So maybe start your own SNC. Cobble it together with whomever you want. Perhaps it won't start until 8:30 p.m. like ours because of all the kids. Maybe create a MNC or a WNC or a standing breakfast date on Thursdays so regular you have "a table." Whatever the opposite of fancy is, that's what this should be (90 percent of our SNC dates are in pajama pants). This requires your hottest commodity: time. So give it. Create margin for it if necessary. Remember the theology: The love of God and people is the whole substance of life. Nothing is more important. This is sacred work and very much counts.

When my online world has gone off the rails and all the Internet chatter is too much and I feel lonely and isolated, nothing fixes me like sitting on a porch with old friends, Texas country on the speakers, real life taking its rightful place again.

So here is my invitation to establish your own SNC . . . traveling evangelist optional, although I highly recommend the handbells.

CHAPTER 17

Quirky

People, I have issues, and it is time to air them. I'm plagued by some idiosyncrasies—certain quirks, if you will. I exhibit a few behaviors that cause people to say, "Really? Get a grip." I'm daring to believe you do also, and please write to me about them, because nothing fuels our eccentricities more than another human saying, "You think that's weird? I've saved all my toenail clippings since 1991." Okay then.

1. Kid Body Regulation

I'm not a hovering mama at all. My kids slide down banisters and build skateboard ramps and shoot each other with airsoft guns. I parent by saying, "Don't cry if you get hurt. Or cry in your room where I can't hear you."

But two issues qualify me for Most Neurotic Mom: my kids' sleep and body temperature.

Since the day they were born, I've been a sleep Nazi. I count their hours. I watch the clock. When someone with credentials said, "Children need ten hours of sleep. Believe me . . . ," I did. *I believed.* My life goal for them is twelve hours a night. I spaz out when bedtime boundaries get pushed: "Oh my word. It's 10:13 p.m. and Caleb is still up. Might as well keep him home tomorrow, because he can't function when exhausted." I am a freak about a good night's sleep. A complete weirdo.

Also I have a very strange fixation about their body temperature. Are you hot? Are you cold? Are you feeling chilly? Are you overheating? Do you need a coat? Where is your coat? Give me your coat. Are you hot? Take off your undershirt. Do you need some water? Are you out of water? Did you drink some water? Do you need to sit in the shade? Do you need to sit in the sun? Do you have enough blankets? Is this blanket too heavy? If you get hot, push this blanket down. If you get cold, here is an extra blanket. Are your hands cold? Are your feet hot? You need a hat. Put on this hat. You can't go out if you don't wear this hat. Take off your hat; it's too hot outside.

After I asked about Ben's heat level twenty-eight times at his soccer game, my friend Tonya was like, "Oh my gosh, Jen! Crazy alert! Leave him alone! You are freaking me out." It's compulsive. We own eighteen reusable water bottles; I just counted. I worry the entire month of August when youth football teams start conditioning in pads. It is so stressful.

I don't care a whit about other issues—for example, safety or ingesting poisons. My kids could jump from a second-story window onto a mattress while testing the feasibility of wind-resistant capes, and I would only worry if they were too hot or if it was too close to bedtime.

2. Musical Immaturity

For nearly my entire adult life, I've lived in Austin: Live Music Capital of the World. We are chock-full of serious musicians and indie singer-songwriters. We have actual producers and artists in our immediate friend circle. I can hear interesting, creative music any night of the week at two dozen venues. Austin hosts ACL and SXSW, two of the best music festivals in the country. Musical taste matters here and is evaluated as a potential character flaw.

I love Top 40.

Like, love it. The sillier, the boppier, the more likely a twelve-year-old girl has a poster of the band, the higher the song is on my Love List. If the band appears in *Tiger Beat*, I'm down. Every song I love ends up on a Kidz Bop CD. My musical preferences are fully unsophisticated. My friends groove to bands called My Morning Jacket and Fleet Foxes, discussing songwriting and creative brilliance. You know what I love? A sixteen-year-old covering a Bruno Mars song on *American Idol*.

Yes, I turn off most raunchy fare, and even I cannot listen to Ke$ha. But Flo Rida? Get in my ears. Don't mind me while I dance and sing at the top of my lungs. Whatever. *I don't even care. Make me throw my hands in the a-yer, a-yer, a, a, a-yer!*[1]

3. Noise Pollution

This is unfortunate, because I've put five kids in this family, but I have an issue with sound. I call it Noise Pollution, and it makes me a little bit of a crazy person. White background noise makes me unravel like a lunatic. My family has been carrying on—going about their business, living a normal life—when all of a sudden, with no warning indicating an impending meltdown, I've flown into their midst like the Wicked Witch snatching remote controls and turning off every beeping, clicking, humming, buzzing, ticking electronic offending me, screaming at everyone with my crazy eyes. Usually, six bewildered people gape at me with open mouths, as it appears the punishment did not fit the crime.

Except that it *so* did.

The sound trapped in my car has actually made me consider sticking knitting needles into my eardrums. Once on a long solo road trip, the unceasing noise caused such despair that I pulled over on I-35, locked my children in the car, walked twenty feet away, and sat in the grass bawling while my kids pressed their faces to the windows mouthing, "Mommy! Mommy! What are you doing, Mommy?!"

I cannot write a word, not one, with a decibel of sound in the room. I need a dead-silent house to eke out a ten-word sentence, so when someone who lives here (who doesn't go to school and is sometimes home during the day) in the quiet space keeps asking me *How do you spell "in lieu of"*? and *Did you put that thing in our iCalendar*? and *I'm thinking about getting a new tattoo*, I might come unglued and threaten to move into an apartment. (This scenario is hypothetical.) (No it's not.)

4. Prank Aversion

I love humor. I love to laugh. I love funny, stupid movies. I love funny people. I love sarcasm and banter. I love witticisms. I love comedy. I am a Melissa McCarthy convert and her loyal disciple until death. I believe laughter is the best medicine, and laugh and the world laughs with you, or some such.

But I cannot handle pranks. *Cannot. Even. Handle. Them.*

Remember *The Tom Green Show* and *Punk'd* and *The Jamie Kennedy Experiment*? Those shows almost put me into a coma. When a bunch of people are in on it, and one person doesn't know, and they are forced into an awkward/horrifying/embarrassing/confusing/distressing situation, I start praying for the rapture. My anxiety goes straight through the roof.

When we had massive delays during Ben's adoption, my friend Missy posted a funny video on my Facebook wall every day until we passed court. Her YouTube ministry gave us many gems, like videos of people falling down. (Why is it so funny every time?) But she posted some prank videos, and they drew no response from me. Finally she was like, "What up, Mrs. Ungrateful? That video was GOLD and you didn't even comment!" And I was all, "I just can't do it, OKAY?" *And in a small voice* . . . "I couldn't even watch." Then she was like, "You're weird, weirdo."

Note that if you invite me in on a prank, I am most likely to prematurely yell: "It's not true! She's not really hurt! It's not even your real car! The waiter is an actor! You actually *did* get the job!"

I will ruin the prank. Count on it. And if you pull one on me, you're dead to me.

5. Such Sweet Sorrow

So, I hate good-byes. And not just the legitimate kind, such as when someone moves to Boston or goes home after a visit. I just hate them all. I absolutely slip out of parties like a ninja rather than doing a big good-bye scene. If my purse is in the hostess's line of vision and Brandon won't indulge my dysfunctional exit habits by fetching it, I will leave it behind and retrieve it from her porch the next day. I've received countless texts like this:

Hey! Where did you go?

Did you leave?

What happened to you?

Did someone kidnap you? Are you in a trunk?

Even if I'm 100 percent positive this is the last I'll see you—your bags are packed in your car which is running, all your kids are buckled in, your husband is giving the wrap-it-up gesture, and the moving van just pulled away to your new life in Atlanta—I will say, "Let's just talk later. I'll see you before you leave." I will say this. I will find a way to not have the good-bye moment, even if it is clearly, clearly the good-bye moment.

☙

I recently discovered that some of my "quirks" are actually introverted propensities. I had no idea! When I read Susan Cain's *Quiet: The Power of Introverts in a World That Can't Stop Talking*, I felt diagnosed for the first time in my life. Experiencing sensory overload and crowd aversion (a conundrum for a public speaker), having homebody tendencies, loathing small talk, feeling social anxiety, multitasking poorly, and having an overactive conscience . . . these mark the introvert, and the full checklist applies to me.

Two years ago, I confessed online to hiding in the bathroom

like a weirdo (again) before speaking at a conference, and someone asked if I was an introvert. Of course not, I said. I love people!
I speak in front of crowds! I have a big personality! I'm not shy!
Something is just wrong with me, that's all. A reader put *Quiet*
in my hands and it was like looking in a mirror. Every tendency
came into focus. I'd just never read the research.

It was terribly liberating, because I quit trying to overcome
my personality. The ugly self-talk stopped and I gave myself permission for quiet and silence and privacy. I finally acknowledged
my social limits and decided there was no shame in protecting
my energy since I just have a lower threshold. (My friend Sarah
is a classic extrovert, and she bounds out of bed every day thinking, *Is everyone already awake? Did they go to brunch without me?
Did I miss a conversation? Who else can join us?* Bless.)

I am a high-functioning introvert, and people constantly
disbelieve my diagnosis. I call as my witness, Your Honor, the
conference speaker perched on a toilet in the bathroom. Let the
record show that she operates better on the stage than the lobby.
I can deep dive with someone on a porch for hours, but walking
into a party of strangers is a fate worse than death. (I retain the
extrovert's flair for exaggeration.)

Interestingly, I married an extrovert. Brandon is a ver-
bal processor who finds his opinion by talking it out, and he
extracts energy from virtually every social setting. He has a
lot of words and a high threshold for activity. When I read the
chapter in *Quiet* on conflict resolution between introverts and
extroverts, I thought Susan Cain had spied on us. It was shocking how by-the-book we handle conflict from opposite camps.

She described a rhetorical couple, "Greg and Emily," and a typical scenario between them:

> When she and Greg disagree, her voice gets quiet and flat, her manner slightly distant. What she's trying to do is minimize aggression—Emily is uncomfortable with anger—but she *appears* to be receding emotionally. Meanwhile, Greg does just the opposite, raising his voice and sounding belligerent as he gets ever more engaged in working out their problem. The more Emily seems to withdraw, the more alone, then hurt, then enraged Greg becomes; the angrier he gets, the more hurt and distaste Emily feels, and the deeper she retreats. Pretty soon they're locked in a destructive cycle from which they can't escape, partly because both spouses believe they're arguing in an appropriate manner.[2]

You guys, this is *exactly* me and *exactly* Brandon, and this was our twenty-year predicament. This single paragraph was cold water on a hot day. I absolutely believed something was horribly wrong with Brandon in conflict and he concluded the same about me. This explanation in *Quiet* (plus the next ten pages, which I highlighted entirely) didn't change our temperaments, but it fostered understanding and helped us meet closer in the middle. Anger shuts me down, and shut-down behavior makes him angry; so now he tries to come down from the rafters and I try to stand up off the floor. We still have about a 50 percent failure rate, but at least arguments make more sense.

Marriage is so easy.

We parent three extroverts, one introvert, and one ambi-
vert who can't pick a lane. Understanding their personalities is
incredibly helpful as parents. We've learned to tailor conflict
resolution, activity levels, and personal interaction to each kid.
Connecting with my introvert is too easy ("Let's lie in the grass
and read all day." "Yay!"), but I sometimes struggle parenting
my extroverts, because their constant interaction and movement
is so encompassing. We recharge differently—they need more of
everything and I need less of everything. This personality gap
can be so defeating, because I feel like *not enough* and make my
kids feel like *too much*. When I lock down from NCF (Needy
Child Fatigue), we all lose.

I learned to access my village, and it made an enormous difference. I had many mothers and my kids do too. Good friends
invite my extroverts to high-energy activities and theme parks.
(Deliver me, Lord.) They supply loving interaction and new
conversation outlets. My kids' aunts and grandmas engineer
sleepovers and one-on-one quality time, lending fresh interested ears to all the words and feelings. This has the dual effect
of filling up my kids' tanks so I can fill up mine.

I've also learned, as in conflict resolution, to meet somewhere in the middle. No mother should cater to an extroverted
kid 24/7, but no child should feel like a burden. Peace lives somewhere in between. The sensory seekers can learn restraint,
and the overstimulated mama can dig deeper. This is good for
everyone and lifts the cloud of frustration. My extroverts are
sufficiently charged with manageable activity; it's not feast or
famine here. Something in the middle is enough. It also helped

to explain my introverted side to the kids. Although my live-wire children don't share my non-talky book-reading needs, as with anything, they can better respect what they understand. It is good to say: *This isn't anything you do wrong at all. It's just the way Mom fills back up.* This loosens the shame that plagues kids and parents who are wired differently.

There is hope for families filled with introverts and extroverts! We can love each other and stretch in healthy ways and practice empathy every single day. I'll close with encouraging research by developmental psychologist Avril Thorne, as explored by Susan Cain in *Quiet*:

> The most interesting part of Thorne's experiment was how much the two types appreciated each other. Introverts talking to extroverts chose cheerier topics, reported making conversation more easily, and described conversing with extroverts as a "breath of fresh air." In contrast, the extroverts felt that they could relax more with introvert partners and were freer to confide their problems. They didn't feel pressure to be falsely upbeat. . . . Extroverts need to know that introverts—who often seem to disdain the superficial—may be only too happy to be tugged along to a more lighthearted place; and introverts, who sometimes feel as if their propensity for problem talk makes them a drag, should know that they make it safe for others to get serious.[3]

Wonderful . . . but don't expect me to start saying good-byes.

CHAPTER 18

Difficult People

Writer's note: This essay discusses dealing with your average, run-of-the-mill, high-maintenance person. It is not appropriate for abusive or violent relationships. If you are in an abusive relationship, please seek counseling and intervention.

Getting older bonus: enjoying the No Drama Force Field I've vigorously erected. I once tolerated melodramatic, high-maintenance garbage, but I've pretty much culled those relationships. Mainly because I am not thirteen and this is not middle school. It is dramatic enough to fit into my jeans every morning; ain't nobody got time for nonsense. I've had friends who flourish on conflict and nonstop drama, and—how do I put this nicely?—I am entirely over it.

To be clear, every human has some drama. We all take a turn in the Crazy Seat. If you breathe air, you are entitled to the occasional meltdown, regrettable public rant, obsessive self-absorbed season, or time in the gutter. (Last year in the middle of a book release, show premiere, and two back-to-back trips to Africa, my bestie finally said, "Jen, I cannot hear one more word about your stress level. I will slap you across the face if you say another thing," and I was all, "I JUST HAVE A LOT OF FEELINGS RIGHT NOW!" Melodrama has a shelf life, people.)

This discussion features two categories of people: The first involves chronically high-maintenance folks who thrive on conflict and attention. This behavior goes beyond a season; it is compulsive. If there is no discord to bemoan (also known as *life*), they create some. These are usually one-sided relationships in which that person possesses all the problems, issues, and losses, and you rarely—if ever—receive reciprocal care. It is all them, all drama, all the time.

Or maybe a relationship has a darker underbelly. Someone constantly subjects you to shaming or guilt-mongering, if not overtly then passive-aggressively. Perhaps someone is simply unsafe; they cannot be trusted with your story, privacy, or honesty. When "friend time" consistently feels like a beatdown, it's time to reevaluate. This isn't complicated: a friend should behave like a friend, not a critic, cynic, gossip, mother, doubter, or hater. There are enough of those; no need to invite them over and feed them lunch.

What separates this group from the next is one word: *optional.* We have no obligation to endure or enable certain toxic relationships. The Christian ethic muddies these waters because we attach the concept of "long-suffering" to these damaging connections. We prioritize proximity over health, neglecting good boundaries and adopting a Savior role for which we are ill-equipped. "Who else will deal with her?" we say. Meanwhile, neither of you moves toward spiritual growth. She continues toxic patterns and you spiral in frustration, resentment, and fatigue.

Come near, dear one, and listen: You are not responsible for the spiritual health of everyone around you, nor must you weather the recalcitrant behavior of others. It is neither kind nor gracious to enable. We do no favors for an unhealthy friend by silently enduring forever. Watching someone create chaos without accountability is not noble. You won't answer for the destructive habits of an unsafe person. You have a limited amount of time and energy and must steward it well.

There is a time to stay the course and a time to walk away.

There is a tipping point when the effort becomes useless, exhausting beyond measure. You can't pour antidote into poison forever and expect it to transform into something safe, something healthy. In some cases, poison is poison, and the only sane response is to quit drinking it. This requires honest self-evaluation, wise counselors, the close leadership of the Holy Spirit, and a sober assessment of reality. Ask: Is the juice worth the squeeze here? And sometimes it is. You might discover signs of possibility through the efforts, or there may be necessary work left, and it's too soon to assess.

But when an endless amount of blood, sweat, and tears leaves a relationship unhealthy—when there is virtually no redemption, when red flags have frantically waved for too long—sometimes the healthiest response is to walk away.

Assessing a relationship as worthy of the toil is a lost skill.

Our culture doesn't value safe boundaries as it should. We criticize the ones who quit, pulled out, drew a line in the sand, the ones who said, "No more." We often think they should've tried harder, stayed longer. We imagine this indicates flimsy loyalty. Surely we'd have done better in their shoes.

But when we are locked in a toxic relationship or community, spiritual pollution can murder everything tender and Christlike in us; and a watching world doesn't always witness those private kill shots. Unhealthy relationships can destroy our hope, optimism, gentleness. We can lose our heart and lose our way while pouring endless energy into an abyss that has no bottom. There is a time to put redemption in the hands of God and walk away before destroying your spirit with futile diligence. Sometimes the bravest thing is to stop fighting for something that is never going to produce a winner.

The most poisonous relationship I can remember broke apart a few years ago. Although in the first "optional" category (eventually), this association was characterized by abusive control, shaming, and bullying. After the bond inevitably shattered into a thousand pieces, I didn't possess a forgiving, gracious thought for a solid year. I was so poisoned, it took years to detox. I had let it go on too long. That relationship did real damage to my soul, and I still battle cynicism I can't entirely shake. I should have walked years earlier.

Jesus modeled this behavior. Without so much as an apology, He told His disciples to "shake the dust off your feet" when encountering hostile people (Matt. 10:14). Jesus put great spiritual responsibility on individuals, and His *move on* vibe cannot be denied. He didn't baby-talk people into healthy choices. He said, "Whoever has ears, let them hear," without so much as a coddle (Matt. 11:15). Jesus was tender toward brokenness but impatient toward egotism.

There is a second, more challenging category: non-optional difficult people. This involves folks like bosses, mothers-in-law, next-door neighbors, coworkers, spouses, children, fathers. The No Drama Force Field is trickier here. The truth is, we can't cull every difficult relationship. That is not real life. Fortunately, we can jettison some and should, but often these people sign our paychecks or birthed us, so they are here to stay.

How do we handle difficult, high-maintenance, or unsafe relationships that must remain?

A good starting point is grace. Not superficial, sentimental fluff but the tough, dig-under-the-surface brand. If a difficult relationship is permanent, grace will grease the wheels. Most thorny people are thorny for a reason. It doesn't excuse bad behavior, but understanding early injuries or hidden wounds cushions blows. It is no free pass, but empathy is a powerful tool toward forgiveness and patience. If we must stay the course, compassion helps us weather the road.

What is this person's trigger? What is his hot button? Where did this behavior originate? Was he abandoned? Abused? Did she struggle? Was she grieved? What makes him scared? What does she fear losing? What is he trying to prevent? What scenario sets her off and why? What sin is he battling? What approach backfires every time, and is there an alternative? Are there painful areas to avoid?

How can you best love this person in the fragile places?

Obviously, you cannot fix someone. You're not a therapist but simply an observant, discerning companion. Life is severe and coping is harder for some than others. We can make the journey trickier or easier, smoothing the path with grace or complicating it with more obstacles. This person is here to stay for the foreseeable future or forever, so he is a necessary member of your tribe. You can exercise compassion without enabling misconduct.

I have a challenging kid; I'll call this child "Kid" because I am a creative writer. Kid was born with an intense temperament. All feelings are big feelings: big anger, big sadness, big happiness, big fear, big reactions. Kid is incredibly sensitive, which has its beauty and its downside. An ordinary scenario for most children can be tremendously emotional for Kid, which creates much drama in the house (as if we weren't already up to our eyeballs in drama). Intensity of any kind puts Kid into fight-or-flight mode, where the coping mechanisms are supertenuous. We ask, "How can we best love this kid in these fragile places?"

Aggression backfires every time. A firm hand on the arm is catastrophic. A raised voice means full shutdown. Kid needs time and distance to regulate, and no amount of forcing the issue works. For Kid, twenty minutes alone is a magic bullet. We've learned we can still parent and discipline without eliciting belligerence. Brandon and I don't bargain or abandon leadership; we simply regard Kid's triggers and hasten resolution.

When we have multiple options, choosing the approach that promotes healing *and* maturity makes sense. I consider Paul's instruction often: "If it is possible, as far as it depends on you, live at peace with everyone" (Rom. 12:18). If I can foster a more peaceful encounter, if there are several means to a similar end, if any measures exist toward goodwill, I should choose them. These become paver stones, one by one, moment by moment, until we've strung together fifty healthy steps and created a better story.

Boundaries come after grace, because compassion minds the fragile places but boundaries keep them from compromising the rest. Brokenness may have legitimate origins, but left unchecked, a wound becomes infected and poisons the whole body (and subsequently, everyone around). Wounds must be attended to heal. With an unhealthy limb, the rest of the body overcompensates through manipulation, aggression, or blaming. Boundaries here are kind. Better to apply direct pressure to the wound than pretend it is well; this may get worse before better, but it is way of healing.

Here is a boundary for beginners: You are worthy of basic human respect just because you are alive. No one should demean, despise, mock, or humiliate you. You should not stand for that behavior. That is not the way of Christ, neither on the giving nor receiving end.

The trick about boundaries is that they must be about you, not the other person. News flash: We can't control people. It is so aggravating! Boundaries assume all offensive behavior will continue for the projected future. You are not altering someone else's conduct but clarifying what you will not put up with. Let's go back to Kid:

Bad boundary: "Kid, you do not get to lose your mind and scream at me!"

Good boundary: "You can be as angry as you want, but you'll do it in your room. If you break something, you will replace it. We'll talk when you've calmed down." (End of scene. No pleading or negotiations. You are calm. You are Mother Teresa.)

Bad boundary: "Stop mocking every word spoken at this table! You're ruining dinner!"

Good boundary: "If you mock one more comment, you'll finish your food in the kitchen while the rest of us enjoy family dinner." (Mother Teresa voice.)

Bad boundary: "I told you five times to do your laundry! Stop ignoring me!"

Good boundary: "You will now do your laundry and mine. No screens until it is all washed, folded, and put away. I expect you to obey the first time." (Do not engage Kid's inevitable anger and mock shock. You are ice water. You are an ice-cold Mother Teresa who just outsourced her laundry.)

This puts responsibility where it belongs: on the offender. If difficult people scream *jump* and we keep saying *how high*, why on earth would they stop? If your mother criticizes your finances but you keep disclosing your budget, you forfeit the right to cry foul. If your boss humiliates you in front of coworkers and your response is to try harder, make your peace with this treatment.

When consequences of poor conduct affect the offender rather than the offended, this is the path to spiritual maturity. *This is so big.* God designed mankind to learn from a sow-and-reap rhythm. Natural consequences are an incredible teacher.

This is how we are transformed. We lie in the beds we make. But craving harmony, we allow all sorts of mistreatment; we reap what *others* sow, robbing them of instruction and absorbing the shock instead. We prioritize keeping the peace over confrontation, but the result is more suffering, not less. Allowing someone to wound you repeatedly is not a kindness.

To some degree, people will treat you however you let them. Consider the bully who takes a blow to the jaw and never bothers *that* kid again but moves on to a weaker target. However, if enough weaker targets push back, eventually that bully becomes a boring accountant who should skip his ten-year reunion. When people are forced to reap what they sow, the benefit of consequence is appropriately placed, and health and healing become possible.

You have permission to walk from certain toxic relationships. Note: Do this well. Don't fire parting shots across the bow. Doing so creates more losers, and you're better than that. Go gracefully. Take your dignity and self-respect and precious humanity, and be proud of yourself one year from now. You don't need to be proven right; validation is not the highest stake. You'll never regret parting with grace, but you might deeply regret burning a bridge that might one day be safe to venture back over again.

And for non-optional tough relationships, engage your empathy first. If you haven't done this, you have no idea how much healing God can manage even if the other person does not change one bit. Give grace a chance to smooth the path; it is a powerful tool in God's hands. Within the context of compassion, create good and right boundaries for everyone's benefit. Let natural consequences be heard and felt; this is also a powerful tool in the hands of God. If spiritual maturity has its way, you'll both be healthier in the end.

And if the No Drama Force Field produces zero measurable results, and all of your relationships remain in disarray and these people collectively are dysfunctional morons and no one can get anything right . . . well, as the cult horror movies from the '80s warned, "Maybe the call is coming from inside the house."

I mean, we are obviously not difficult, but people we know are. We'll pray for them.

CHAPTER 19

Bonus Supper Club Menu

This was one of my favorite SC menus by Aaron who is so naturally talented in the kitchen, I want to stab him. This meal was so delectable, I lost consciousness. Recipes by Aaron, parenthetical commentary by me because I am here for you.

౸

Braised Lamb Shoulder and Onion Sauce over Herbed Mashed Potatoes, and Warm Chocolate Cake with Milk Jam

Serves 8

(Make the lamb and sauce one or two days ahead of your dinner party. Your main dish will be done already. You're welcome.)

(Don't fret about "lamb." This is like cooking pot roast. Relax.)

The Lamb (Day Before)

5 lbs. of trimmed boneless leg of lamb

4 cups vegetable stock

3 onions, coarsely chopped

7 celery stalks, chopped

5 peeled carrots, chopped

12 sprigs thyme

5 sprigs rosemary

2 heads of garlic, halved

salt and pepper

Preheat your oven to 325 degrees. In a big stockpot, season your lamb with salt and pepper, sear on all sides until brown, and transfer to platter.

In the same pot, add some oil and cook celery, carrots, and onions on medium-low until caramelized. Add the vegetable stock, bring to a simmer, and return lamb and juices to the stockpot (one-pot meals make me SO HAPPY). Add water to cover the lamb. Add the thyme, rosemary, garlic, and more salt and pepper, then bring to a simmer. Cover and put in the oven for four and a half hours.

Let your lamb cool completely in the stock, then transfer the lamb to a platter. Strain the stock and discard your solids (or feed them to your happy chickens). Return lamb to stock and refrigerate overnight. (Just keep it in the same pot with a lid, because you'll use it again tomorrow. ONE POT MEALZ FOR LYFE!)

The Onion Sauce (Day Before)

2 sticks unsalted butter

6 garlic cloves, thinly sliced

1 shallot, thinly sliced

1 bay leaf

2 onions, thinly sliced

1 tsp. orange zest

1/4 tsp. cardamom

1/4 tsp. cinnamon

1/4 tsp. cloves

1/4 tsp. turmeric

one bunch flat-leaf parsley, chopped for garnish

Heat butter in a large saucepan (two sticks . . . you read that right . . . LIVE A LITTLE). Add garlic and shallots until brown, then remove to a plate. Reduce heat to low and add onions. Cook for an hour or so until caramelized. Stir garlic and shallots back into the onions, and add your spices and bay leaf. (You're done here. Put this in Tupperware once it has cooled, and it will be ready to go tomorrow.)

The Chocolate Cake (Day Before)

(I cannot even with this. Serve this dessert and become a legend, Home Cook. Start this also the day before and you will practically have nothing to do on Dinner Day.)

One box of chocolate cake mix
Some butter
Some sugar
1 cup toasted pumpkin seeds, for garnish
1 cup fresh raspberries, for garnish
Some mint leaves, for garnish

Make a normal chocolate cake from a box. (Amen and hallelujah. Ain't nobody got time for homemade cake.) After it cools completely, slice it into one-by-four-inch strips, around the size of a finger. (That is Aaron's description, and I think it is VERY CREEPY.) Roll each cake strip in sugar. Store all these in a closed container until tomorrow.

The Milk Jam (Day Before)

2 cups whole milk

1 cup sugar

1 cup crème fraîche (to be added on Dinner Day)

Boil milk and sugar over medium heat. Reduce to low, simmer, and whisk until it thickens and turns light reddish-brown and measures about a cup. Store in the fridge. You can make this up to a week in advance.

Finishing the Braised Lamb (Dinner Day)

Skim the fat from the stock. (It should be solidified on top like a gross layer of Crisco. If you are like my grandma, save this for future flavoring.) Remove the lamb, shred into large chunks, and set aside. Put the pot on medium heat and reduce the stock to about three cups. Once reduced, add back the shredded lamb and 1/4 cup of the onion sauce over low heat. Keep this simmering until you are ready to serve.

Plate the lamb over the mashed potatoes and drizzle with remaining onion sauce and chopped parsley. (YOU ARE A HERO. Your guests will praise you at the city gates.)

Herbed Mashed Potatoes (Dinner Day)

The herbed mashed potatoes aren't complicated. Just make regular mashed potatoes: peel, cube, boil, and mash your potatoes. Add lots of butter, cream or milk, and salt and pepper to taste. Add a big chopped handful of the herbs you used in the lamb—rosemary, thyme, and parsley. The end.

Finishing the Chocolate Cake and Milk Jam (Dinner Day)

Right before serving, sear the sugared cake fingers (ugh, Aaron) in a hot skillet with butter. Sear on all four sides. This will just take a minute.

In a bowl, whisk together the milk jam and the crème fraîche.

To serve, stack two or three warm cake fingers (oh my gosh I need counseling now) on each guest's plate. Pour the milk jam on top and sprinkle with the toasted pumpkin seeds, raspberries, and mint leaves.

⌒ꝺ

This meal is a home run, dear ones. It is the most comforting of food. Serve it with a simple green salad and your people will feel immeasurably loved and cared for. Lamb loves wine, so pair it with a Bordeaux, a spicy Cabernet, or a robust Chianti Classico.

CHAPTER 20

Thank-You Notes (Part 3)

Thank you, Young Twentysomething Celebrities, for reminding me why I never want to be in my twenties again. In fifteen years you will no longer make sex tapes, drink vodka six nights a week, forget your panties, or start asinine Twitter fights. (Did you forget your twelve million followers can read the words you write when you hit Publish?) I'm sorry to tell you the pictures you've posted will always exist, but at least when they are still circulating during your forties, you'll be reminded of how nice your breasts looked back then.

Thank you, Four-Year-Old Daughter, for yelling at two-year-old sister: "Are you going to listen to me? Or do you want TO DIE ON THE CROSS FOR YOUR SINS!?" You have destroyed my Good Parent image while also proving the dangers of bad hermeneutics.

Thank you, Maternity Yoga Pants, for the extra-wide elastic band in your waistband and for the great job you do keeping my baby bump in check, especially since it's been five and a half years since I had my last baby.

Thank you, Dry Shampoo, for letting me have forty more minutes of sleep this morning. I know I didn't shower. You know I didn't shower. But no one else needs to know I didn't shower. (A specific shout out to Dry Shampoo for Brunettes, because now I can use you without looking like my Grandma Peck.)

Thank you, To-Do List, for going along with it when I add things to you I've already done, just for the satisfaction of crossing them off. I don't expect you to understand my neuroses, but I appreciate your live-and-let-live policy. I have so few things left. Give me this small victory. Yours, Completer of Meal Planning, Post Office Trip, E-mails to Teachers re: Child's Absence Last Monday, and Boot Resole.

Thank you, *Caillou*, for having a nonphonetic title so my son cannot look you up on Netflix.

Thank you, Looming Book Deadline, for giving me eyes to see dirt in weird nooks and crannies of my house, which must be cleaned immediately. You've also helped me understand the urgency of organizing my pantry, sorting my Instagram pictures into folders, and seeing what might be on sale at Anthropologie .com. Finally, you've rekindled my relationship with all social media outlets, so thank you for creating such passion for anything other than you.

Thank you, Target, for depressing us by stocking your store with adorable jackets, sweaters, and boots in August even though it's still a hundred degrees outside and won't even dip into the seventies until November. This seasonal tragedy is not your fault, but we don't need cute knit legwarmers in September. We still need a swimsuit section. Please download a weather app and send it to your buyers. Sincerely, Every Fall-Loving Texan Crying in Her Tank Top at Halloween.

Thank you, Siri, for never understanding anything I ask you and searching the web for sites that could probably get me arrested. My husband's name is not Rendon, I did not want directions to "The Ass House," and I did not want to call my pediatrician at 12:30 a.m. (I said "daughter," not "doctor," and now she is very, very sorry she gave me her cell number that one time. I'll never get quick antibiotics again.) Dang it, Siri.

Thank you, Pinterest, for feeding my split personalities by inspiring me to bake a triple chocolate mousse after an intense ten-step ab workout. I also appreciate your numerous outfits and matching accessories laid out as inspiration for regular shaped women, especially the size 0 jeans and skintight tank tops that were meant for newborn babies. If I squeezed into that outfit, I would look like a sausage trying to escape its casing. I'm not sure you've ever actually dressed a human woman, but hey—the outfit looks real pretty laid out on the ground like that.

Thank you, Automatic Flushing Toilets. My undersomethings really needed a quick spritz of nasty as I attempted to dismount you this morning. The backs of my upper thighs even got in on the action, which was a real surprise for them, and not like a "Hey, I booked us a trip to Cancun" surprise but more like a "Guess what? This is not just a toilet but a poop bidet. You're welcome." Sincerely, Lady Who Just Screamed in the Airport Restroom.

Thank you, Texting, for ensuring that, if executed well, I'll never have to talk on the phone again in my life. This is like a stay of execution for introverts. I'd also like to take this time to thank Emojis, for helping me express my innermost feelings via cats, crying cats, devil cats, and women dressed up as cats. You really "get" me. However, I would take a lovesick cat over talking words every day of the week. (Fist bump!)

Thank you, Autocorrect, for making me appear simultaneously like an English professor and a perverted gangster. I didn't actually want to *punch* my friend's baby but rather *pinch* her. Who punches a baby? I'm not on roids! You have some serious issues. Sincerely, That's Not What I Meant.

CHURCH, CHURCH PEOPLE, NOT-CHURCH PEOPLE, AND GOD

CHAPTER 21

Poverty Tourism

Brandon and I had an illuminating conversation with a local leader in Ethiopia. He led a church and accompanying nonprofit, and a western group discovered his work. Eager to do good and champing at the bit to do it internationally (so sexy), they started visiting his children's home once a summer. Because they failed to listen, learn, and enter a foreign culture with humility, not valuing the local leader's expertise, cultural intuitiveness, and authority, they visited his community annually with the pre-determined mission to paint the children's home. Again.

So before they arrived each July, the children rubbed the pristine walls with dirt and debris so the Americans could repaint and feel good about their "helpful yearly trip."

We can do better than this.

This is a complicated conversation for both participants and critics of short-term mission trips to tread thoughtfully. I graciously invite you into this discussion because surely, as we engage this world, we aim to help and not hurt. Worth noting, good intentions are virtually guaranteed here. Motives aren't in question but methods—our respect of indigenous cultures, the local effects, and long-term sustainability. Effective short-term mission trips exist, and good questions, humble self-examination, and deference to locals will get us there.

Let's start where we should always start: the local community we wish to serve, whether international or domestic. This should not be an afterthought to our trip details. No community is an agenda, an outlet, or a lesson, and its people are not photo ops. Poor people are not dumb, clueless, helpless, or ignorant; they are resourceful and resilient. Any wrong thinking that casts them as folks to pity and fix needs eradicating. We do not start with our trip; we start with the people.

Anytime the rich and poor combine, we should listen to whoever has the least power. Rich people are conditioned to assess the world through our privileges. The powerful tend to discredit or ignore the marginalized perspective because we can. We are shielded from the effects of a lopsided equation; we reap the benefits not the losses. We don't mean to do this (or even know we do), but we evaluate other communities through the lens of advantage assuming we know best, have the most to offer. In doing so we unintentionally elevate our perception.

Every missional conversation should begin with local leaders, local families, local ministries, and the local perspective. *Tell us about your community. What is the history? What have you overcome? What are you still battling? How are you leading your people? What has worked? What has failed? What is the local vision for community development? Who else is leading well? How is the partnership with your government? What systems are broken in your community? What is your greatest need right now? What is your greatest strength to that end? Where is God moving? How can we support what you are already doing? How could we best serve you? What "help" has actually hurt and how can we avoid that? Is a short-term team of any value to you, or could we better partner from afar?*

In contrast, take a snapshot of many short-term mission trips (and thanks to my missionary friend Jamie Wright for this perspective):

Invite anyone who can afford it to a poor country or community; raise tons of money; collect supplies to transport (rather than in-country purchases to spur the economy); make matching T-shirts with graphics and slogans like, "Making Disciples and Feeding the Hungry: Fill-in-the-Blank Church Goes to Mexico!" (and be sure to wear them in front of undiscipled, hungry Mexicans so they understand your charity); release unskilled laborers on a construction project of your choosing (I know I'd want twenty-five teenagers to paint my house or build a whole structure rather than a skilled local contractor); do some western-themed evangelism; put unknown burden on local leaders as they host (and forget to ask missionaries how they truly feel about most short-term trips); go home conflicted but grateful for abundance; and change your Facebook picture to one of you with that kid you "loved."[1]

Stay with me. I've participated in and even led this exact trip, so I am a humble, repentant learner too. May I explain the harm here? First, the benefit to the team trumps the benefit to the community. It does, even if we believe we are serving well. Sure, we go home moved and thankful (at least for another month or two), but to what end? If the goal of "exposure to poverty" outpaces humble, deferential, strategic work in an impoverished city, we turn people into props for our own betterment.

The poor are not blind to this either. Folks know when they are an object lesson, even inadvertently. Yes, the rich people may be "learning a lot here," but what are the poor learning? That we are so grateful not to live there? That we weigh their circumstances with obvious, kind pity? That we will fix things since they are clearly incapable? These effects are common, yet most impoverished people are too polite and deferential to challenge the earnest team members who are relishing their trip.

While we compare our lifestyles to theirs and come out on top, they also compare theirs to ours and come up short. They absolutely perceive the Haves who helicoptered in to "love on" the Have-Nots. *Challenging our wealthy perspective cannot be our chief goal.* We mustn't use the sorrow of another to reinforce our joy, even unintentionally. Of course we want to battle entitlement and indulgence, but not at the expense of another soul. There is no dignity in this. It strips people of pride, patronizing them and robbing their leaders of authority. It creates burden and dependence and can be entirely humiliating.

If you feel your "but . . ." rising up, I fully identify, but my argument should be considered, especially when it keeps showing up in the field. For me, a shift in worldview was the result of years of conversations with missionaries, local leaders, poor community members, and nonprofit directors. I read their books and learned best practices, trusting their authority and expertise in their own nations and contexts. I traveled internationally with them or worked alongside them domestically as a learner and saw a completely different model than what I knew. I'm watching this conversation change, with great effect, and I'm learning that "what I get out of a trip" isn't the highest aim.

When the minority voices say the same things, those with privileges should listen. We should triage our own experiences as people with power and humbly heed those on the other side. While many short-term team members are undoubtedly transformed, that is not reason enough to continue harmful work. It just isn't. Personal growth will be a residual effect, but it should be a secondary benefit to those reaped by the local community.

So what does a good short-term mission trip look like?

It clearly begins in the mission field with local leaders and nationals internationally or even in the impoverished sections of our own cities, as I mentioned. We come alongside the folks who live there as humble learners, outsiders to their culture, history, systems, and practices. We listen. That is all we do at first. We take copious notes. We defer. We delete every preconceived idea about helping, serving, traveling, or engaging. Oh my gosh, we put our paintbrushes down. (The world is so done being painted by the American church.)

We look seriously at systemic issues in that community. We learn about root causes, broken structures, and societal breakdowns, such as violence and lack of subsequent justice, poverty orphans, the abuse of women and children, economic disempowerment, environmental degradation, educational disparity, maternal health, and nutrition and healthcare. We listen to local leaders on long-term sustainable solutions and engage the discussion with humility. Again, this can be international or local. (Middle- and upper-class America is shockingly disconnected from the plight of the poor in our own country.)

We partner only with local missionaries, leaders, and organizations vested in their town or country. (If you want to serve your city's homeless, start with the folks already serving your city's homeless.) As uneducated, inexperienced outsiders, we must work with people who live and work and breathe the sustainable, holistic health of their community. We need trusted experts here. These trips are too costly—in human and financial capital—to fly halfway around the world to put on a puppet show. High-capacity local leaders who are capable of affecting long-term benefits to their communities are essential. We should be floored by their aptitude and awed by their vision for development, which will include short and long-term goals, measurable outcomes, and educated solutions.

If Americans work with poor communities, the partnership should be long-term (outside of emergency relief). We do not blow in and out, nor do we invent our own trip then find some random missionary to host us. If we go, let's be prepared to *go back*. Prioritize the long-term health and dignity of the community, and to that end, relationships are critical. In Haiti with Help One Now, the nonprofit I serve, a local pastor we work with said, "After the earthquake, hundreds of churches came with promises and pledges, and virtually none came back." I bet those churches fondly remember that one trip to Haiti while the locals feel abandoned.

We cannot go a mile wide and an inch deep in community development, because these are people, not projects. Pick your mission and invest with all your guts. Exchange names, numbers, e-mails, pictures, letters—evidence of commitment. Elevate local leaders and prioritize their authority year after year, because development is not stagnant and requires constant evaluation. Local leaders should only encounter respect, partnership, and loyalty.

(Side note: You want to meet the child you sponsor? GO. That is not short-term missions; that is visiting a beloved child or family. I've seen your pictures and letters taped to their walls. You are precious to them and would be a welcomed guest. Bring your kids. Bring the letters you've saved from your sponsored child. If your trip is born out of relationship, then it will be a treasure to all involved.)

We should set aside the value of our experience entirely. That benefit will come anyway, so don't worry about it. With intelligence and critical thought, we can consider a community through research, partnership, listening, and learning. Ask new questions and raise the bar, understanding how some intervention can be neutral at best, destructive at worst—and surely we want better than both. Consider the most broken elements of a community and partner toward urgent issues that affect lives rather than frivolous projects that waste money, time, resources, and opportunity. Remember the poor are capable, smart, actual people, and treat them with the respect they deserve. Battle every patronizing, pitying thought that robs them of humanity.

We can indeed help instead of hurt, and it is noble, necessary work. May we not send one more orphan group to muddy the church walls so we can paint again in July. Instead, may we come alongside that brave, courageous local pastor and ask, "Good brother, how can we help you empty this orphanage over the next twenty years?"

CHAPTER 22

Dear Church . . .

Reader, brace yourself: Brandon and I have been on a church staff since ages twenty-one and nineteen respectively. When I recall leading those youth—*who were basically our peers*—I can only be thankful God's grace and twenty years likely erased anything we taught, bless our hearts. I am also the daughter of a pastor, albeit a very rogue pastor, but still. I've had a behind-the-curtain perspective on church leadership my entire life.

Brandon and I grew up Southern Baptist; flexed early ministry muscles at a "liberal Southern Baptist church" (pretty sure this is an oxymoron; the biggest scandal involved lady deacons so, you know, *clutch your pearls*); moved on to a big, cool "seeker church"; then landed in the random embrace of the Free Methodists. Brandon has led teenagers, college students, adult discipleship, events, men's ministry, and now a whole church. I study Anglican theology, read prayer books by priests, serve alongside friends from the Word and Faith movement, and secretly envy the charismatics. I love the liturgy of the Presbies and can party like a Catholic. I've taught in every sort of sanctuary and worshipped with bands, choirs, dancers, and quartets. I pretty much love all of the church. Each expression is a bit of a hot mess, but bless her, she's *our* mess.

I have much hope for the church, even as she sometimes gives me indigestion. I realize many beloved readers were hurt terribly under the steeples, and a bunch left and a bunch more want to. Some of you never tried it at all, because the church is so, you know, churchy. Organizing something as mysterious and marvelous as God's family is just hard. I can't think of a group that requires more grace.

I have a few thoughts, first for church leaders and second for church people; I am weirdly protective of both because I *am* both. I love the girl on the sixth row who barely got in the door, and I love the pastor who studied all week while caring for his unwieldy flock. At the end of the day, both groups are just ordinary people who struggle and sin and sometimes act courageously and sometimes act horribly. The curtain is much thinner than it appears. Here goes.

꩜

Dear Church Leaders, You are so dear to me. You've been extra fathers and mothers my whole life. I know the vast, vast majority of you are good people who love God and want to be obedient. As with any profession, the loudest lemons get the attention, but most pastors are men and women of honor. I respect and love you immensely.

Listen, you should take a vacation. I know you need one. Consider a sabbatical if you've been working nonstop for twelve years. I'm serious. The stats are not on your side and should be heeded: 90 percent of you work between fifty-five and seventy-five hours a week; 70 percent of you fight depression; 80 percent of you believe ministry has negatively affected your families; and only 10 percent of you will retire as a pastor. For Pete's sake, 70 percent of you don't have one close friend.[1] This is not good. With numbers like these, could we reimagine some things together for the health of your churches, your families, and your own souls?

Maybe we start here: 90 percent of you believe you inadequately manage the demands of your job, and half of you are so discouraged, you would abandon ministry if you had another job option.[2] Any career in which 90 percent of the laborers feel "not enough" indicates a fundamental problem. Surely this is not the church Jesus intended. When your nearly unanimous cry is "I cannot do it all," maybe the answer is simple: you actually cannot do it all and should quit trying.

It's not working, you are dying, and people are leaving anyway.

I wonder if the American church is positioned poorly? If church structure—which is geared toward meeting every need, developing everyone spiritually, and organizing all inward and outward ministry—results in a 90 percent fail rate, perhaps we should reevaluate. When a faith community is church-centralized, the staff is expected to take full spiritual responsibility for people, which is well beyond their capacity. Sure, a few churches are so enormously staffed that paid pros can keep the plates spinning. But most churches are small or midsized with a modest staff that cannot handle such demands.

I wonder if a "Come to us and we will do it all, lead it all, organize it all, calendar it all, execute it all, innovate it all, care for it all, and fund it all" framework is even biblical? It sets leaders and followers up for failure, creating a church-centric paradigm in which discipleship is staff-led and program-driven. This slowly builds a consumer culture wherein spiritual responsibility is transferred from Christ-followers to the pastors, and this is a recipe for disaster.

The numbers expose this effect on you, but there is also a detrimental impact on your congregation and ultimately your community. When you tell your people, "Come Sunday for worship, Tuesday morning for Bible study, Wednesday night for Community Group, Thursday night for Awana, Friday night for a service project, and Saturday afternoon for leadership training," it is defeating. Intentionally or not, it develops a culture in which discipleship is measured by attendance.

It communicates that all of this *stuff* counts the most.

Ironically, while you work yourselves into an early grave, your people feel overextended too. Unsurprisingly, you turn on each other. Each group feels resentful; pastors wonder, *What more do these people want from us?* and the church folks wonder, *What more do these pastors want from us?* This approach is not making disciples but is creating a lose-lose situation where no one feels they can deliver.

And what of your community? When your people are expected (overtly or not) to invest mainly in staff-led ministries, you'll fail to launch missionaries into your city—not because your people don't care but because *they have no more time.* Although data is hard to solidify, the church is losing roughly fifty thousand people a week. The reasons are numerous, but the *number-one factor* cited is too many family responsibilities, which lead to overloaded schedules.

This is happening, so maybe the church can embrace new forms, new measures of success. Encourage more decentralization built on mission and flexibility, creating margin for busyness while still championing the kingdom. As leaders, let's widen the definition of *what counts.* Does an informal gathering of seven people discussing God bear less weight than a church service? If a family gives two hours on a Tuesday, is that less meaningful than two hours on a Sunday? If a Christ-follower spends hours engaging his searching friends over wine and hummus, we can't also expect three church programs to legitimize his investment.

Ironically, the more responsibility people take for their spiritual development and their neighbor, the healthier they become—also, less resentful of the church, less dependent on programming, and less reliant upon pastors. This frees up the staff for more reasonable roles, and the people to be good neighbors.

I am suggesting this, pastors: Offer less, empower more, validate nontraditional ministry, and set a new standard from your pulpit. Preach this, teach this, celebrate your unconventional servants from the stage, bang the drum for simple missional lives, and if the machine is killing you, stop feeding it. Doesn't that sound like a wonderful relief? This could be profoundly good for you and your membership.

One more thing: The numbers tell us you suffer in private and struggle in shame: 77 percent of you believe your marriage is unwell; 72 percent only read your Bible when studying for a sermon; 30 percent have had affairs; and 70 percent of you are completely lonely.[3]

You guys are a mess! Which makes sense because you are human, like every person in your church. You are so incredibly human but afraid to admit it. So few of you do. Clearly, pastors struggle mightily; yet we rarely hear this from the pulpit. The average person sits in church weary and burdened, with no idea her pastor deeply understands her grief. So everyone keeps pretending.

You are afraid to be transparent, sometimes with good reason. Not every congregation is safe for an honest leader. Some churches prefer the illusion, because leaning into a pastor's humanity is hard and uncomfortable. But fear is a terrible reason to stay silent. Fear is a terrible reason to do anything. It isn't a trustworthy motive and it doesn't ever lead us to wholeness. Scripture tells us plainly that fear is not of God, so operating out of self-protection takes us further and further away from a life of the Spirit, and that is an impossible fracture for any pastor to navigate.

This is more than a neutral omission. Power and authority can corrupt the dearest soul, and leaders who lack transparency are more susceptible to leading abusively. Pride knows no boundaries, and when pastors self-protect from the pulpit, they tend to become manipulative, fear-driven, and controlling. If you are infallible on Sunday morning, then you start believing you are infallible Monday through Saturday too. People become commodities to protect the façade, and the risk of exposure and loss can turn shepherds into tyrants.

Nearly 40 percent of the dechurched cite mistrust for their pastor. I beg you to get in your pulpit and tell the truth. About yourself. Vulnerability is absolutely transformative and creates more trust, not less. Your people are broken and hurting, and instruction without identification deepens the shame—both yours and theirs. What a blessed relief when a pastor confesses his or her humanity. When you present yourself onstage as inhuman, people put inhuman expectations on you everywhere else. You are more than a leader; you are also a brother or sister, and the family needs more truth-tellers. To return to Brené Brown and her book *Daring Greatly*, "If we're going to find our way out of shame and back to each other, vulnerability is the path and courage is the light. To set down those lists of what *we're supposed to be* is brave."[4]

Here is how James put it (and I love this paraphrase in *The Message*): "Are you hurting? Pray. Do you feel great? Sing. Are you sick? Call the church leaders together to pray and anoint you with oil in the name of the Master. Believing-prayer will heal you, and Jesus will put you on your feet. And if you've sinned, you'll be forgiven—healed inside and out. Make this your common practice: Confess your sins to each other and pray for each other so that you can live together whole and healed" (James 5:13–16).

In other words, say the truth about how you are doing, even if your name is on the marquee. If you are hurting, say it. If you are sick, say it. If you are sinning, say it. This holy practice of confession creates wholehearted and healthy faith communities. What incredibly important theology. The path to healing feels terrifying, church leader; but this scripture is either true or it isn't. Confession saves the truth-teller and truth-receiver, because God is liberated to move. I believe Him for this. I've seen it. Give a heady sermon and folks are moved, but give a vulnerable sermon and they are set free.

A healthy church begins with its leader, and folks rely on the compass of your identity. Be well, good pastor. Bench yourself awhile if you need to. Speak emancipating, petrifying truth in front of your people; give this biblical instruction a chance to work. Evaluate your church culture and decide if you are making disciples or consumers. Please be tender with yourself and your church; everyone, including you, is fighting a tough battle. Let's remove the heavy yokes we've put on one another while trying to get this church thing right. Give shocking grace and permission to your people, and they will give it back.

Let's make our faith communities beautiful again using the unsexy, ordinary tools that have always worked: truth, confession, humility, and prayer. They are surely not fancy, but they save and heal.

Even you.

☙

Dear Church People, First let me broaden the definition of who "church people" are. How about church people, former church people, and potential church people? It's a fluid category, so all of you can just gather round. You are so incredibly dear to me. I particularly like the prickly folks on the outer edges, but I was raised by church choir ladies with casseroles, so I have big heart-space for all the concentric rings.

Let's go ahead and address the "stuff": Church is a teeny bit crazy. I know this. I am this. Approximately four of you don't have church baggage. These wounds range from "This feels irrelevant and weird" to "This place crushed my soul." I've experienced both, so I promise to be a gentle friend.

When I was a kid, I thought my parents knew everything because they were parents. I was unclear how information about All The Things had been transferred to them, but I was certain they were in possession of it. They seemed very old and parent-ish, and I believed they were fully certain about our world and its happenings. What was their real life? I have no idea. I thought they existed to parent us.

When I realized my parents were in their twenties and thirties when they raised us, I freaked out. Babies! They didn't know everything! They weren't sure about anything! I know because I've completed my twenties and thirties, and we don't know jack. We use smoke and mirrors while we figure it out behind closed doors. Plus, sometimes we are cranky and tired of parenting and just want to go to our own mom's house and take a nap.

Our kids don't know we are real people, but they'll figure it out one day.

I think many church folks feel this way about pastors. We perceive them as experts in everything, super-special and somehow different (better) than us; and we suspect they are always certain when we sometimes doubt. Plus, their job is to pastor us, and that is the beginning and end of them. Just as kids don't think of parents as human people, we assume pastors exist to pastor.

Dear ones, pastors are so terribly human. Did you read the previous letter? Most are struggling, lonely, overwhelmed, and sad. They battle the same sin and tendencies you do, and they are equally susceptible to life's quicksand. Their hearts are no less tender and their souls are no less vulnerable. Sometimes they are not sure. Sometimes they project authority while trying to figure it out themselves. They can blow it as husbands, wives, parents, and friends, and they often do. Their list of "shoulds" can be paralyzing, and most pastors live with a chronic sense of disappointing people.

Now obviously they accepted a pastoral role, which comes with responsibility. They'll answer to God for their care of souls, and trust me: That reality is sobering when "being human" does not excuse them from humble, diligent leadership. To whom much has been given much will be required, and that certainly applies to human care. Pastoring is no role to accept lightly.

But I wonder how much expectation is placed on mere men and women? They have the same twenty-four hours a day, the same basic capacity, and the same "life outside of church" as anyone—spouses, soccer games, fishing trips, dinners. Some of this is their doing, I know. They've given you the impression they can meet all your needs (perhaps having no needs themselves). Maybe they have a class, a staff member, and a curriculum for everything under the sun, so everything seems in hand. Plus, if they aren't transparent, their pedestal is protected.

And this pedestal thing. What a nightmare. Please don't feed into this. It has created some monsters. When church is less like a family and more like an enterprise, its leaders act less like pastors and more like commanders. This puts everyone in danger—the leaders and the people. Spiritual abuse thrives where pastors are untouchable and people are commodities. No one intends this, but absolute power corrupts in every human environment. The right things become too small—humility, Jesus, ordinary church folks, simplicity—and the wrong things become too big—the pastors, toxic hierarchy, success, appearances.

Church in general bears a heavy burden. After forty years under the steeples, I am convinced we want more than church was designed to provide. Unreasonable expectations leave pastors constantly depleted (or power drunk), and people constantly disappointed (or codependent). The early church involved small, organic communities who gathered around tables, lived simple lives on mission, and loved God and neighbor. That was kind of it. The first believers assembled for renewal and teaching and dinner and togetherness. It was so basic and lovely. Everyone pulled weight, pitched in, pressed into God. The early church wasn't fancy or entertaining, impressive or complicated, but it managed to take the gospel to the whole world.

I don't know your feelings about church, but what if you freed up your pastors to be ordinary men and women, your church to be a simple family, and your life to be for loving God and people?

I don't mean to minimize church damage; that pain is real, and wounds from supposedly trustworthy people cut deep. I know this personally. Don't hear me say, "A pastor or church person or church hurt you but they are just human so lah-dee-dah." One's humanity is never a license to injure, especially by those in leadership. Like any organization, church has mostly wonderful, dependable leaders and some abusive, manipulative ones. I wish we could shield the church from our humanity, but alas, the two are hopelessly linked. Church leaders are regular old sinners but should still be vetted with discernment. We don't carelessly place our families under spiritual authority. (My checkpoints, in order: 1. humility; 2. transparency; 3. integrity.)

But under a humble leader, in the fold of ordinary folks who love God and each other, the church can be the safe family Jesus dreamed up. It really can. Without unrealistic expectations foisted on one another, we are unbound to create a beautiful little community.

You are capable of a Spirit-filled life on mission without constant church management. Does that free you up at all? Does that help you free the church up too? You've got the goods: Here is your Bible, there is your neighbor, you know the prayer words, you have eyes to see your city, and the Holy Spirit dwells within you. The kingdom tools are yours already: Scripture, a smart mind, a kitchen table, capable hands, the capacity to study and learn, a heart full of Jesus, a porch, people to learn from, people to love. Honestly? Life is convoluted but the kingdom is simple. We overcomplicate the ways of Jesus.

Love God, love people.

Act justly, love mercy, walk humbly.

Treat people as you want to be treated.

If you want to be great, be a servant.

It really is simple—a pure kingdom lived in ordinary ways by ordinary people. Let's unshackle each other's hands a bit. Our pastors and churches teach and gather us, challenge and launch us, but no church supersedes you living your beautiful, valuable life on mission. You fulfill an extraordinary role through ordinary means, and no leader or church can do this for you. There is no whole without the pieces.

If you assume an obedient life requires a thousand moving parts, a bunch of church programs, an international movement, a big fancy ministry, or a giant platform, let Jesus' description of the kingdom relieve you: *small, invisible, humble, tiny seeds, mostly hidden.* Faithfulness is not easy, but it is simple. You are already able, already positioned, already valuable in your normal life on your normal street next to your normal neighbors in your normal work. The priesthood of the believer is real.

Also? Church people are regular old sinners too. If I could fix this, I would. As it turns out, the church isn't a gathering of shiny new pennies. It lets anyone in the door! All sorts of hooligans fill the sanctuaries: kind and good ones, angry and cynical ones, mean and judgmental ones, smart and funny ones, broken and sad ones, weird and awkward ones, precious and loving ones, scared and wounded ones, brave and passionate ones, insiders and outliers, newbies and lifers and trying-one-more-timers. Just a whole bunch of human people. Every church has all these folks. It is just the hottest mess, but clearly you belong here because everyone does. Find your little faith tribe (it exists) and learn to love it with all the grace and humility you can muster.

If we allow people to be human and God to be God, the

church has a fighting chance. If you show up brave and true, and leaders show up brave and true, if you own your place and I own mine, the kingdom will break through in every possible way. God is big and good enough to lead us all, and together we just might see His kingdom come on earth as it is in heaven.

CHAPTER 23

If Social Media
Were Around

Way back in ye olden days, I scrapbooked. (Can you even handle this? Isn't it so unlike me?) Well, I did. I took twenty-four unfocused pictures per roll (this was "rolled-up film" we used to put inside "cameras"), developed them at Walgreens, and ended up with four mediocre shots that I cut into triangles and stuck in lignin-free albums on themed pages. Besides chopping every existing baby picture of my children into heart shapes covered with stickers (I need therapy), the biggest downside was no way to publicly baby-brag. Because social media wasn't a thing. (Young ones, we communicated on what we called "home telephones" and wrote what were known as "letters" and recorded Christmas morning on "giant camcorders only grown men could lift.")

Now here in the new world, I've been a full-blown Facebook freak since Mark Zuckerberg decided money was more important than awkwardly meeting coeds. Once he opened the gates of his creation, I quickly became that mom who whined about her schedule, shared photos of *So You Think You Can Dance* parties, and ~~spied on~~ bonded with my teenaged children.

I won't lie: I love the social media. It has connected me, reconnected me, and introduced me to some of the funniest, smartest, most creative, interesting people on Earth. It has also devoured one zillion hours I should have used to write, exercise, and keep my children from hitting each other with sticks. It's a place of incredible affirmation (Oh! They like me!) and incredible disparagement (Oh! They despise me!), so I have a love-hate with the medium. But I'll always drop whatever I'm doing to watch videos of cats running on wood floors.

I also love diving into the posts of a past month or year, becoming instantly awash in memories, cackling over photos, and occasionally deleting a too-honest status. (PSA: Info on ovulating does not belong on Twitter. You're welcome.) Unfortunately, electronic reminiscence is only possible as far back as 2004 when social media became a thing. Before that, we only have grainy star-shaped pictures in scrapbooks. The digital barrier to my past leaves me asking big questions like, "Would Simon Le Bon have followed me on Twitter?" or "How many likes would my eighth-grade graduation picture have generated?" or "Would Tinder have destroyed the delicately balanced dating infrastructure that marked Oklahoma Baptist University in the early '90s?"

In a world where everything is connected by Bluetooth and a blender can MAKE SOUP (VitaMixers, I'm *this* close to your bandwagon), surely someone will invent a way to dump pre-2004 shoeboxes, diaries, and photo albums into some digital wood chipper to reverse engineer our social media lives. When they finally do, I'm fairly sure my early social media history would look something like this:

 Jen King @JenKing—January 25, 1984—Houma, LA
Church bought dad a computer! It's like the Year 2000! He has no idea how to use it, but still. It is tiny—only 27lbs. #FORTRAN #DadStopCussing

---

 Jen King @JenKing—September 30, 1984—Houma, LA
Coach Dad made me pitch again since Jennifer S. couldn't hit the side of a barn. Face filthy because DIRT STICKS TO TEARS. Covered in burnt orange dust. #WorstColorEver

---

 Jen King @JenKing—May 22, 1987—Houma, LA
Mom & dad at church for HOURS. I'm home watching the kids. UGH. #ChildLabor Lindsay won't stop asking for Cajun food. I get it. We live in Houma. #MakeItYourself

---

 Jen King @JenKing—April 13, 1989—Haysville, KS
Had the best time at youth group! #WednesdayWarrior Won the skits with my Paula Abdul imitation. #StraightUp

---

 Jen King @JenKing—January 27, 1991—Haysville, KS
Working on cheer competition routine. Jennifer M. late *again*. She HAS to take this seriously! THIS IS SO IMPORTANT AND MATTERS FOREVER.

Jen King @JenKing—October 13, 1991—Haysville, KS

I HATE typing class. When will I ever use this stupid skill? Like I'm going to type for a living. #asif #Apple2eBLAH

 Jen King @JenKing—May 16, 1992—Haysville, KS

Accepted to Oklahoma Baptist University! Not sure where Shawnee is, but it's gotta be better than Haysville. #Freedom #TheGreatAdventure #SaddleUpYourHorses

 Jen King @JenKing—July 28, 1992—Haysville, KS

Mom took me shopping today and bought me overalls! Can't wait to wear them at college! One strap down of course. #WillSmithStyle #FreshPrincess

 Jen King @JenKing—August 16, 1992—Shawnee, OK

First day at OBU! Got my RX7, a new perm, and THERE ARE BOYS EVERYWHERE! #ForTheLove Can't wait to call Mom collect and tell her everything!

 Jen King @JenKing—October 21, 1992—Shawnee, OK

That Brandon guy keeps showing up everywhere I am: the mail room, whatever church I'm trying out, the cafeteria. I call him the #PoloShirtBoy

 Jen King @JenKing—February 14, 1993—Shawnee, OK

Brandon and I write letters every day. We will NEVER stop doing this. This will always be our thing. I FINALLY FOUND THE LOVE OF A LIFETIME. #FireHouse

Jen Hatmaker @JenHatmaker—December 31, 1993—Wichita, KS

Our wedding was DREAMY! Colors: forest green and burgundy, of course. Tea-length bridesmaids dresses. No alcohol at reception. #Baptist #AlsoIAm19

 Jen Hatmaker @JenHatmaker—December 12, 1994—Shawnee, OK

Celebrating 1st wedding anniversary studying for a current events quiz. New constitution in Ethiopia. #Whatever #NoIdeaWhereThatIs

 Jen Hatmaker @JenHatmaker—May 14, 1996—Shawnee, OK

I think mom is genuinely surprised I graduated OBU today and I am #NotPregnant #TeacherNow

 Jen Hatmaker @JenHatmaker—June 8, 1996—Tulsa, OK

Hired to teach fourth grade at Jenks East in Tulsa! I get $75 to spend on supplies for the whole year! Should be plenty! #fancy #CarsonDellosa

Jen Hatmaker @JenHatmaker—September 10, 1996—Tulsa, OK

Bet my students & parents LOVE these weekly Social Studies packets! Talk about quality learning time together! Can't wait till homework with my kids one day!

Jen Hatmaker @JenHatmaker—June 23, 1997—Tulsa, OK

School's Out! Just in time to chaperone Brandon's youth group at camp. #NoRest Who sells 1-piece bathing suits in Tulsa? #ModestIsHottest

Jen Hatmaker @JenHatmaker—July 1, 1997—Tulsa, OK

Youth camp was amazing! Lots of tears on Prayer Candle Circle Confession Night and 79 rededications. We are all #JesusFreaks now. #DCTalk

 Jen Hatmaker @JenHatmaker—September 4, 1997—Tulsa, OK

I'm not saying these fourth-graders make me sick, but this is the third day I've puked before homeroom. Ugh. This flu is making my boobs hurt too. #weird

 Jen Hatmaker @JenHatmaker—September 20, 1997—Tulsa, OK

Brandon just TOTALLY does not understand me and teaching is SO HARD and if I am crying I DO NOT WANT TO BE FIXED. #FeelSadAboutEVERYTHING

 Jen Hatmaker @JenHatmaker—September 30, 1997—Tulsa, OK

You guys, fell asleep ON MY DESK today. Students woke me up. Omg. It's like I can't get past 6:00 p.m. Looked up breast cancer on Microfiche. #symptoms

 Jen Hatmaker @JenHatmaker—October 9, 1997—Tulsa, OK

YOU GUYS WILL NEVER GUESS WHAT I'M ABOUT TO SAY IN A MILLION YEARS. I'm serious. No one saw this coming . . . #YouHaveNoIdea #Stunned

Jen Hatmaker @JenHatmaker—March 21, 1998—Tulsa, OK

If my belly gets any bigger, I might need my own zip code. If Hasbro sold a home c-section kit I'd buy one RIGHT NOW. #TheScaleMakesMeCryTears

Jen Hatmaker @JenHatmaker—April 9, 1998—Tulsa, OK

RT @BrandonHatmaker WE MADE A BABY AND THE BABY GOT BORN! HE IS GOING TO LIVE WITH US!! #GavinJoseph

Jen Hatmaker @JenHatmaker—July 11, 1998—Tulsa, OK

My tiny baby just destroyed the entire backseat with a poop explosion. It was otherworldly. Throwing away car seat. #NoRecovery #IDriveASewer

Jen Hatmaker @JenHatmaker—August 13, 1999—Corpus Christi, TX

Teaching first grade (????) at Luther Jones in Texas! First day: wrote my name on board & a kid said, "Miss, we can't read." #OMG #SendHelp

Jen Hatmaker @JenHatmaker—September 2, 1999—Corpus Christi, TX

Texas puts stars on like, everything. Highways, hamburger wrappers, tattoos on their actual bodies. I'm never drinking this Kool-Aid. #ObsessMuch

Jen Hatmaker @JenHatmaker—September 19, 1999—Corpus Christi, TX

Ohmystars, if I don't get a Wendy's cheeseburger in the next five minutes I AM GOING TO COMMIT ACTUAL MURDER.

Jen Hatmaker @JenHatmaker—September 28, 1999—Corpus Christi, TX

Cannot quit crying. It's like, the world is just so harsh. What's the point? No one even cares. We're all just going to die and no one will remember us. #sad

Jen Hatmaker @JenHatmaker—October 3, 1999—Corpus Christi, TX

Like I'm supposed to believe a $4 pregnancy test. Like God would give me two babies in diapers at once. #ForTheLove

Jen Hatmaker @JenHatmaker—February 13, 2000—Corpus Christi, TX

Bought a small fixer-upper. If my nesting instincts weren't raging, renovating this house with Brandon would be a nightmare. #NeverAgain

Jen Hatmaker @JenHatmaker—May 23, 2000—Corpus Christi, TX

Dear Lord RT @BrandonHatmaker If there's a way to love a baby girl more, I want to see it. I am the champion wife picker and baby maker. #SydneyBeth

Jen Hatmaker @JenHatmaker—July 15, 2000—Corpus Christi, TX

The house is done, Corpus Christi is beautiful, Brandon's job is great, Sydney is sleeping through the night. #Perfection #StayForever

Jen Hatmaker @JenHatmaker—October 1, 2000—Corpus Christi, TX
Guess who's moving to that hippie-infested Sodom and
Gomorrah known as Austin. That would be us. Me=Jonah,
Austin=Nineveh #FakeHooray

 Jen Hatmaker @JenHatmaker—March 3, 2001—Austin, TX
DEAR AUSTIN, BE MY BOYFRIEND. Breakfast tacos. Music
everywhere. Cool people. Did I mention breakfast tacos?
#MyTown #InLove

 Jen Hatmaker @JenHatmaker—July 2, 2001—Austin, TX
Bought season tickets for TX football instead of paying
electric bill. Dispensing Austin propaganda. #Koolaid
#MoveHereFamily #IHaveYourGrandchildren

 Jen Hatmaker @JenHatmaker—August 24, 2001—Austin, TX
School is back in session and I'm not. @BarlowTrina
medicating my teacher withdrawal symptoms with bootlegged
mimosas. #ChurchStaffBoozeBan #SAHMS

 Jen Hatmaker @JenHatmaker—October 16, 2001—Austin, TX
Brandon found me, Gavin, and Sydney crying on the kitchen
floor today. HE DOESN'T KNOW MY LIFE. I miss work that
pays. I'm a terrible mom. Boobs hurt. #sad

Jen Hatmaker @JenHatmaker—June 4, 2002—Austin, TX

Really? RT @BrandonHatmaker We recently celebrated Jesus leaving the tomb. Today, my new son, Caleb, exited the womb. #ThreeAndDoneForSure

Jen Hatmaker @JenHatmaker—May 22, 2003—Austin, TX

3 kids at home. Leading another Bible study. Hubby working 70 hrs/wk in ministry. How can I fill that 5 minutes of free time daily? #SarcasmFont

Jen Hatmaker @JenHatmaker—June 30, 2003—Austin, TX

Thinking about turning my Bible study stuff into a . . . thing. Like a pamphlet? Maybe a booklet? Does Kinko's bind? Can I borrow a typewriter? #NoComputer

Jen Hatmaker @JenHatmaker—January 22, 2004—Austin, TX

LIFE IS ABSURD. People want to publish my booklet. I think I have one book in me and #ThatIsIt before I go #BackToTeaching. #LeaveWritingToBethMoore

Jen Hatmaker @JenHatmaker—February 17, 2004—Austin, TX

I'm really enjoying this productive nonstop writing, but I'm just going to take a peek at this Faceback thing to see if I know anyone . . . #shortbreak

CHAPTER 24

Thank-You Notes (Part 4)

Thank you, Sick Husband, because what I mistakenly thought was just your cold with a minor fever is apparently something closer to onset Black Plague with a side of liver disease. According to your indications, you're presenting pandemic symptoms from Europe, circa 1300 AD. We should alert the CDC! I mean, sure, I pulled off carpool, dinner, homework tutoring, and four kids' practices last week when I had strep and the flu, but you just stay in bed with your scratchy throat. *We don't want to infect the children.*

Thank you, Spam Writers, because I've been curious to hear from Slirped_Up_Butt_Juice on my post about parenting ESL children. I love how you keep the conversation naturally flowing by writing: "Greetings,My name is JOHN, i am highly interested in buying your {what you want to sale} from you ,I will like you to give me the FINAL ASKING price and the lastes condition, I have a liable shipper that takes goods care of all my shipping. So pls email me back so that we can conclude about it. Bay

Bay, John." Perhaps the English acquisition strategies I discussed in the article could be of assistance to you. Thanks anyway, Uninterested in Becoming a Mystery Shopper in Pakistan.

Thank you, Department Stores, for the flickering fluorescent lights, dingy yellow wall paint, and adjustable mirrors in the dressing room where I try on bathing suits. You are why I drink.

Thank you, Reply-To-All Replyers, because I treasure getting fifty e-mails that all say, "Congratulations!" or "I'm praying!" or "LOL" or "Thanks a lot, Obama." Really, my delete finger is now strong enough for all those moves I learned in self-defense class. You have potentially saved my life. (Side note: Thank you, Dad, for those helpful forwards about gun control. You've really nailed the chief political concerns of your three grown daughters.)

Thank you, Trampolines, Bounce Houses, and Peppy Aerobics Classes, for the reminder of birthing multiple children. If somehow the lack of sleep, missing brain cells, or haggard mommy appearance didn't do the trick, you display my new lack of bladder control. No, I didn't want to wear those pants all day. Let me search through my mountainous laundry pile and grab some swimsuit bottoms to throw on since the twenty pairs of underwear I purchased before 2003—when I cared about underwear—are all dirty.

Thank you, Spotify, because if it weren't for your sneaky Facebook updates, my friends wouldn't know I just listened to *Jock Jams*. Sincerely, A Mom Just Getting Ready to Rumble.

Thank you, Sandwich Artists at Subway, for always wearing gloves because, really, I feel much better about the integrity of my cold cut sub after you opened and closed the oven door, wiped down the counters with your dirty rag, and lifted the trash can lid five times whilst crafting my sammie. Because you have on your sanitary gloves. It's fine. Whatever. It's not like that ham was freshly butchered from a locally-sourced pig by a trained chef. There's not even a kitchen up in here, unless you count a walk-in freezer. As far as I can tell, the only "cooking" done here involves a microwave and toaster. Just give me my six-inch. I take vitamins.

Thank you, Book Club, for allowing me and my friends to maintain the façade that we are still cool and smart and read books, when really we just drink wine and eat. Please don't tell our husbands because we make it sound like this is purely intellectual stimulation.

Thank you, Facebook Quizzes, for helping me identify my Disney princess spirit, my old-person name, my mental disorder, and the color of my soul. All in one evening. Best, Ariel Harriet Schizophrenic Mauve.

Thank you, Skinny Jeans for Men, for making guys believe they look like Justin Timberlake when most of them more closely resemble Gru from *Despicable Me*.

Thank you, Disney, for making my daughter think the only good beginning to a pretend plotline is to kill off the mom. You also introduced my young son to the jungle boy Mowgli. He needed a good excuse to run around in his underwear with easy access to his man-parts. Sincerely, Mom Who Loves to Say, "Stop Touching Your Penis."

Thank you, ABC Family Channel, for your "family-friendly" programming. I always let my kids tune in to your shows featuring liars, whores, and murderers. I'm not sure what your definition of "family-friendly" is, but a high school plot to kill the homecoming queen's deaf and secretly gay stepsister is pushing it. Tighten it up, you guys.

Thank you, Taco Bell, for knowing one hundred sauce packets and zero napkins are the perfect number of things to put in my bag.

Thank you, Rotisserie Chicken and Frozen Vegetables, for being the last-minute dinner that says I care. A little.

Thank you, All Baby Clothes Ever. You're so cute and look so innocent, but you're so sly with your snaps that require an engineering degree and your socks that ARE NOT MADE FOR BABY FEET. You are so cute that by the time my screaming baby is dressed, he's heard more curse words than a Dane Cook special. Thanks, Circo. My baby is so presh looking. What are these random neck and crotch snaps for? Yours truly, Sweaty.

Thank you, School Fund-Raisers, for making my children think they can't live without those twenty-five-cent toys you give out as "rewards" for selling six thousand dollars' worth of wrapping paper and dips and jams. When you invade their school with your loud basketball-arena pump-up music and peddle your wares, this is basically extortion. Every year I have to tell my children that in no context, through no stretch of the imagination, are they actually going to win a limo ride to a Taylor Swift concert by selling candles. Can we just not?

Thank you, Woman Who Does My Nails, for always asking in a sad and not-so-subtle way if I'd also like to get my eyebrows done.

CHAPTER 25

Dear Christians, Please Stop Being Lame

Based on an actual Facebook exchange:

ME: Facebook, I just love you. In the last month together, we've built a tiny home for a formerly homeless resident in Austin, raised 50K for Help One Now, and committed to four hundred new child sponsorships in Ethiopia. What good work for the kingdom. You are amazing. You are my peeps.

RANDOM COMMENTER: So where's the gospel, Jen? I've followed your blog and FB page for several months, and there is NO GOSPEL. I guess I've just "missed it." You have a big following and should take that very seriously. You have a higher accountability and you will answer for your influence.

This makes me want to pack my family and move to Sweden. Honestly, I love Jesus but sometimes His followers give me a migraine. And instead of getting more patient, I'm becoming intolerant. Actually, the whole world is fuming, and that frustration is turning to indifference. *Oh well, another Christian acting like a sanctimonious gatekeeper. What do we care? Onward.*

This is no longer an optional conversation. We are past treating this behavior as we do Crazy Uncle Bob who acts like a racist redneck (but, you know, it's Uncle Bob, and no harm no foul as long as he never discovers social media). The issue is no longer trite or inconsequential. We are losing influence in our culture, and it isn't even a mystery as to why. Folks are explaining plainly why they are leaving faith or are too afraid to come near it. One of the chief reasons is this:

Christians.

I realize the mass exodus is multifaceted and deserves a fair analysis, but the common denominator is so abundant, we have to face it. Particularly since other factors—a postmodern worldview, shifting religious cultures, generational hurdles, changes in the traditional family dynamic—are seismic shifts largely beyond our control. These cultural conversions are happening inside *and* outside of Christianity and are necessary to assess and understand.

But treating each other poorly is not a factor Christians can pass off.

This one hits square between the eyes.

Listen, I realize I am, as my girlfriend calls me, a Christian Crap Magnet (such a lovely term) because a disproportional number of people read my words. I understand that. I do. An extra measure of Christians regularly announce how poorly I am parenting, living, leading, and even cooking. I attract a concentration of criticism, and honestly, I can handle it. I really can. (God worked a miracle in me, a Former Pleaser, so I can get out of bed in the mornings.) I'm not operating out of hurt feelings, dear reader, because most of you are my heart's delight. Plus, you police the crazy for me, so here's a fist bump.

This is way bigger than me. This is my neighbor welling up at my church invitation, saying, "Oh no. I see how Christians talk to you, and you are their poster girl. They would destroy me. I'm terrified of them." This is the next generation weeping for their gay friends and classmates, rejecting the church that maligns an entire community. This is my smart and funny friend who lives in loneliness because her Christian "friends" wounded and shamed her, and she is afraid to try again.

We live in Austin, an incredibly unchurched city that I love. Our community is so secular, I am detached from the homogenous Christian pack and attuned to the outsiders' perspective. (*Outsiders* is a misleading term, as our country is roughly 65 percent unchurched. A better phrase is "most people.") We are in urgent times here. The way of Jesus is not holding, and to assume otherwise is a dangerous lullaby that will rock us to sleep while our communities flounder and struggle. Only determined denial could assess our Christian subculture as healthy.

Because *all is not actually well*, it is time to become humble—loving neighbors and the world that fears and rejects us. This is not about being liked or popular, nor is it some soft gospel that prefers harmony over redemption. Here is the truth: If we are inhibiting others from finding Jesus, this constitutes a full-blown crisis. Ultimately, the rejection of Christians predicates the rejection of Jesus, and if that doesn't grieve us, we have missed the whole point. Jesus tried to impress this upon us. I mean, He was obsessed.

"By this everyone will know that you are my disciples, if you love one another" (John 13:35).

"I in them and you in me—so that they may be brought to complete unity. Then the world will know that *you sent me and have loved them* even as you have loved me" (John 17:23, emphasis added).

The woman at the well.

The Good Samaritan.

Blind Bartimaeus.

The poor widow.

Zacchaeus.

There is a clear correlation between how we treat each other and how a watching world will feel about Jesus. What should our neighbors deduce from our loving-kindness toward one another? One, that we obviously belong to Jesus, because what other explanation exists for such beautiful community? It should be so compelling that others interpret it as otherworldly—*these people must belong to God.* And according to Jesus, God's calling card is love. If folks don't recognize God is good by watching His people, then we have tragically derailed.

Two, that God loves people, because how can you explain

such behavior? *These are beloved people, and if they are emulating their Savior, then this must be a good Savior.* Loved people forgive and encourage, serve and uplift, because they are precious to someone. They live within a ridiculous "others first" paradigm that only secure, beloved people can pull off. God loves these folks well, which makes them crazy kind. How else can we understand this goodness? *And could this possibly mean that God loves me too?*

That a watching world is so far from these conclusions grieves me to no end. How far away is this tangible kingdom? When I ask my non-Christian friends what they conclude by observing Christians, it is so unlike the above description, I could weep for days. Secular culture recognizes our theology, but they are woefully confused about our love—which means we have woefully confused them about our God.

We'll talk about loving our neighbors later, but let's discuss loving each other first. There is a great deal of New Testament instruction on loving brothers and sisters in faith. Every single writer mentioned its gravity. It is not only our testimony, but also our reward. What a treasure we receive alongside salvation! The lonely, the outcast, the sick, and the sad inherit a family. We get mothers and fathers and sisters and brothers. We are welcomed around tables and invited into hearts and homes. We don't labor upon our sickbeds unaccompanied; no tragedy is weathered alone. Teachers, mentors, faithful friends—they become ours. This is part and parcel of salvation. God created a whole family out of us, and we reap the benefits. What insane advantages.

Why isn't this reality for so many?

Since there is an egregious disconnect for so many weary

travelers, can we discuss the breakdown together? We are talking about eternity here—so the situation is fairly dire. Faith, Jesus, souls; this is substantial stuff and we desperately want to get it right. We have this ancient text borne in a culture not like ours, and we want to take the words and stories and do right by them. We want them alive and true in our generation. We want it said of us that we were faithful.

These are noble goals, no question. But from my vantage point, I spot a familiar villain: fear.

We tend to formulize the mysterious, opting for a more manageable gospel than the wild, unpredictable one we have. We'd like one with clearer edges and better boundaries, because who can fathom a Savior born in a barn who washed the feet of His followers before dying for people who hated Him? Who can follow Jesus in the ways He walked? The early church was a hot mess. God's Bible "heroes" were a disaster. Theology was constantly misunderstood after the Nazarene carpenter muddied water that previously had seemed clear.

It is no wonder humanity has long preferred legalism, which involves much cleaner territory. Give me a rule any day. Give me a clear "in" and "out" because boundaries make me feel safe. If I can clearly mark the borders, then I am assured of my insider status—the position I feel compelled to defend, the one thing I can be sure of. I want to stand before God having gotten it right.

This mechanism eventually creates visceral fear: Am I getting this *right enough*? Do I understand God correctly? Is my theology accurate? Am I pleasing God? Am I banishing doubt? Can I defend my positions? Are my talking points sound?

Unfortunately, the easiest path to satisfying answers involves confirming others' position as outsiders. It is a cheap trick, sure, but effective. If I can indict your interpretations and traditions, then my place is better secured. It matters not if these issues are entirely peripheral; just the "rightness" or "wrongness" of them is comforting.

The truth is, God has redeemed the world across cultures, countries, world powers, systems, religious orders, trends, movements, and human hearts since the beginning of time. His ways are entirely outside of our understanding. Sure, I know and love God in my context, because it is the only one I know; and I am grateful He found me here. But He has rescued people in and out of church, in and out of religions, and in and out of traditions since time began. He operates in truly mysterious ways we won't know of until heaven. And we will probably be shocked.

I also suspect "getting it all right" isn't God's highest order. The Bible constantly elevated love over knowledge, mercy over sacrifice. Knowledge is a tricky bedfellow, because it can sometimes shield us from the gospel. Doctrine is tidier terrain than flesh and blood. Surely not one human being ever stood before God having "gotten it all right," anyway. Not one. We don't even know what we don't know. Our blind spots are so terribly blind. Some of the rightest rights turned out wrong. Some of the rightest theologians are on opposite sides of doctrine. Some of the rightest leaders break people in the wake of their intellect.

Could the highest level of "right theology" involve loving God and people like Jesus suggested?

Fear makes us terrible brothers and sisters. We needn't be so right over one another. We should certainly treat each other like family, in any case. Our siblings in Christ don't need another parent; they have God. (Like I tell my kids approximately every second: "If I need your help parenting, I will ask.") The condescending way we speak to each other—correct publicly, nitpick and criticize, question and disapprove, waiving the benefit of the doubt—is just gross. It's why so many observers pass by this family altogether.

As in any family, we have matters to work out. I am not suggesting we abandon difficult conversations or ignore a brother or sister heading toward the gutter. We must teach and lead each other, but it should be faithful, loving work between real-life companions who've earned the right to speak truthfully. It should involve private discussions cloaked in dignity and grace, prioritizing understanding as much as instruction. It should not include smug piety shots that create a victim out of a brother or sister.

I hope the world sees a community with wide-open arms, which comforts and welcomes and seems determined to build one another up. I hope they find us kind and generous, committed and loyal. The church raised me, held me tight, and continues to be my steadfast family; and I haven't the slightest idea where I would be without her. May we show love in big and small ways, and may that love reach people accustomed to being shamed or ignored. The bright stars shouldn't get all the attention; let's search for those whose lights are dimmed, because we are not a tribe of supernovas but of steady, collective light.

Let's treat each other well, making more space for every

sort of ragamuffin. We needn't mistake unity with uniformity; we can have the first without the second. The breadth of God's family is mercifully wide. Grace has no discernment, apparently. Jesus created a motley crew, plucking us from every context and inaugurating a piecemeal clan that has only ever functioned with mercy. We should be grabbing hands, throwing our heads back, and laughing that God saved us all, because surely this is the messiest family ever and He loves us anyway. Our shared redemption should keep us grateful and kind, because what other response even makes sense?

May the world see a thankful, committed family who loves their God, adores their Savior, and can't get enough of one another. This is a story that saves, a story that heals, and the right story to tell.

CHAPTER 26

On Women

Helen, Marie, Ann, Inez, Ruth, Mavis . . . These were my grandma's girlfriends, present in my earliest memories. They all held me the first week I lived. I cannot remember my grandma without them—in her kitchen, playing dominos, vacationing at her Colorado cabin, attending our graduation ceremonies, bringing the swankiest gifts to our weddings and baby showers. Their friendship spanned sixty-plus years around card tables, porches, Formica countertops, and Sanka. Their weathered hands smoothed our hair, rubbed our backs, wiped our tears, and breaded our chicken and fried it in lard.

Judy, Rita, Sandy, Debi, Prissy, Cheryl, Sharon, Melissa . . . These were my mom's girlfriends. They also comprise virtually every childhood memory. We grew up at their houses. I can picture every room in their homes—our hide-and-seek nooks, that one hallway we eavesdropped through the vent, the backyards where we peeled tons of boiled crawfish, the kitchens stocked with Ovaltine and Tab. All kids belonged to all moms and they group-parented us, a loose term for basically keeping us alive back then. These women changed our diapers, drove us to home-coming, and cried at our weddings. Their collective laughter is like a childhood soundtrack.

I grew up with so many extraordinary, ordinary mothers and grandmothers.

It is probably why I value my girlfriends so much, although I didn't know to credit Mom and Grandma until later. In my world, this was how grown-ups did life. You and your best friends handled every matter life slung at you. You jointly raised a bunch of kids, and once they were grown, you still had each other plus an impending slew of grandbabies, sons- and daughters-in-law, and clean homes for the first time in twenty-five years.

Women have been amazing to me my entire life.

Spiritually, I grew up with mixed messages regarding a woman's worth. Church taught that women were great in their place, but that place was pretty narrow. My mothers and grand-mothers were incredibly capable and smart. I never understood their small place in the kingdom when they occupied such enor-mous space in my development. Their collective skill set was stunning: they were teachers, entrepreneurs, business-owners, courtroom professionals, realtors, administrators. They led at home and work, but I didn't see their authority translate to church.

I wish they'd had the permission and influence God is restoring to my generation. I mourn the small platform for their wisdom, because the kingdom needed a larger dose of their leadership. As it is, we are daughters and granddaughters of incredible women, and we get to rise up and carry on their legacy. We stand on their shoulders, and not one modern woman would lead today without the conversations they shaped and the changes they forged. With courage and resolve, our mothers and grandmothers moved the needle forward for women.

God is unveiling women around the world. He always has and continues to work through women and girls, who are half of His church. They are, like men and boys, His image bearers. They are also, like men and boys, gifted, empowered, smart, and anointed.

The underground church in China would wane without women. Women disseminate the gospel in the Middle East under threat of life and limb. Women lead bottom-up social movements combating poverty and pioneer top-down legislation to the same end. They are doing quiet work and loud work, onstage and behind the curtain. There has never been a better time to be a woman!

Although historically oppressed, women have always maintained a dignity that shall certainly be eternally rewarded. The women of the world are brave and responsible. When a woman earns money, it will more likely be spent on her own health and safety, as well as that of her children. For every dollar she makes, she will spend eighty cents on her family's health and well-being (when in contrast, men only spend about thirty cents on their families and are more prone to wasting the rest).[1] Women have held communities together for centuries.

What I am trying to say is this: I think women are amazing. They always have been.

We are such a blessed generation. We don't have to choose

between gentleness and authority, a tension fought in secular feminism. We can have both. We get the victories of past generations, plus the hope of ours. We can provide hospitality *and* declare the Word of God, nurture our households *and* embrace our gifts, set the table of communion *and* the table of theology. I am so grateful my daughters see women leading courageously. They won't battle a less-than status or suffocate their gifts. *They'll just run.*

Sister, come near and listen: You are smart and capable, strong and wise. You are an overcomer, a prized member of the body of Christ. You have so much to offer. You can gather your girlfriend tribe and raise kids together, providing the happiest childhood they ever complained about. You can crack open your Bible and preach good news for the poor. You can model faithful friendship around your table, and you can stretch your hand across oceans to mamas everywhere. You can do small work. You can do big work. You are so able in Jesus, so beloved, so permitted.

If anyone has made you feel invisible or less-than, write a new narrative on your heart. The Bible was used to subjugate women for centuries, but the New Testament reveals women leading the church, prophesying, teaching, and co-laboring with men. Let's flourish under Paul's instruction: "Do your best to present yourself to God as one approved, a worker who does not need to be ashamed and who correctly handles the word of truth" (2 Tim. 2:15).

You are approved.

You are a worker.

You have no need to be ashamed.

You are a truth-handler.

You are a sanctioned, honorable operative in the splendid task of loving God and people. You have a role. Your place is secure. If not you, who? Who else will deliver hope to your people? Who else will embrace the weary and lonely? Who else will teach the good Word and claim its promises? Who else will laugh at the days to come with courage? Who else will raise your children in strength? Who else will take responsibility for your people and your place?

You will.

We will together. We will mother all our children and grandmother all our grandchildren. We will cheer each other on, refusing to speak doubt into our gifts. When you are scared, I will declare, "You can do this." When you whisper a dream, I'll holler through a bullhorn that you are brave and wonderful and important! When I am beaten down, you will remind me that I am an approved worker with no shame; we lift each other's heads and handle truth for one another.

It's time. Don't wait for permission; we've already been given it. Lead, sister. You have authority to use your home as a sanctuary, your hands as tools of healing, your voice as an instrument of hope, your gifts as channels of incredible power. "If your gift is prophesying, then prophesy in accordance with your faith; if it is serving, then serve; if it is teaching, then teach; if it is to encourage, then give encouragement; if it is giving, then give generously; if it is to lead, do it diligently; if it is to show mercy, do it cheerfully" (Rom. 12:6–8).

Let's do this. Let's fulfill the good work we've been commissioned to. Silence any voice that whispers "not enough" and stand in truth as an approved worker. You are. Jesus made you so. If God surveyed the cross and declared it finished, then it wasn't sufficient for everyone except you. If Jesus covered it all, then He covered it all. You are now approved, like it or not. Or as God told Peter: "Do not call anything impure that God has made clean" (Acts 10:15). Okay then. That is pretty straightforward instruction.

If you need to deal, then deal. Wrangle whatever holds you down or holds you back. You are too vital to lose years to regret or shame or insecurity or fear. We are not slaves to those masters; Jesus saw to that. Face your issues with courage, sister, because truth and love win, and you have both those cards to play. Ask God: What lies do I believe about myself? What lies do I believe about You? The Holy Spirit is an incredible leader and healer. Don't shove it down; lay your junk on the table and deal with it. Address the stuff. Forgive, release, acknowledge, confront, feel the feelings, let something go, believe the truth, whatever you need to do. Then dust your hands off and get ready to *go*.

I think we're ready, aren't we? I hear it. The dreams, the visions, the excitement. I am flabbergasted by women everywhere. They are overcoming, enduring, outlasting, shining, leading, risking, showing up, speaking up, standing up. They are chasing down dreams right in the middle of living their lives. I am regularly amazed. This generation is choosing to lift each other up rather than tear down, finding ways to love God and people across generations, cultures, countries, and obstacles. Women are teaching with authority that blows my hair back. We are doing hard things in invisible trenches. We are saying yes when saying no would be easier. We are saying no when saying yes would be easier. We are taking responsibility for our global sisters because enough is enough; we won't sit idly while people are abused, trafficked, sold, and abandoned.

If women indeed hold up half the sky, then let's raise our arms high.

Let's show up for our own lives.

Take all the hard parts—the failures, the losses, the wounds—and give them to Jesus for glory. He makes magic with those, I tell you. Those scars are a gift; they say, "See, I've been there, and here I am still standing and you will too." They become badges of honor, agents of healing.

This really is your one wild and precious life. You matter so much. You are writing a good story for your children. Your community and church need you, your neighbors and family need you, God adores you and Jesus is obsessed with you. Here we are, your community of women running this race together, proud of you, moved by you. We'll stumble; that's part of the course, but we'll leave no woman behind. Our generation will cross the finish line having loved God and people with all our might. We'll have imperfect lives to offer, sure, but I dream of heaven, seeing millions of folks loved by our hands, where hopefully we'll hear: "Well done, good and faithful servants. You sure were fun to watch."

Conclusion

I may have mentioned we have chickens. We moved into our old farmhouse, cleaned out the coop, and now we are Chicken People. (Memo to potential Chicken People: Various predators like to kill chickens, which are not smart enough to get away; so it is advisable not to treat them like pets by, say, naming them McNugget and Teriyaki and Barack O'Brahma like *some* Chicken People who assumed their chickens would live forever. As my son Ben said, "In Ethiopia, we don't cry over chickens." Duly noted.)

Chickens are so funny, you guys. We open the coop door every morning and they sprint out like Flo-Jo. We let them free range all day long, and each one has her own ideas. We have three rogue chickens that squeeze through our gate every day and loiter in our neighbors' yards. They have wanderlust, apparently. They will waddle their weird little bodies a block away, because I guess their fallen sisters weren't a cautionary tale against predators.

Others stick to the same exact pecking path in our yard. We have a whole acre but they keep to the fence line on the south side. One chicken is constantly on top of our cars, outdoor table, refrigerator, and trampoline. Our yard is her Everest.

But no matter where they wander during the day, as soon as the sun starts setting, there they are, all ten of them, back in the coop roosting on their perch, packed tightly together like brave little Chicken Sisters. The day's adventures are done and they are home for the night, snuggled in wing-to-wing, living to see another day. (If you think I'm about to compare women to chickens, you are correct, ma'am.)

When I consider the community of women we belong to, there is no doubt our daily adventures take us all over the map. Some of us live on the edge and venture way beyond "safe" boundaries—predators be darned. Others of us thrive in the constant, steady spaces that have always made sense to us. Still others keep jumping up for a new view, a new perspective, a new perch. Daytime finds us all over the place, diverse, unique, distinct. This is so good, this lack of homogeny.

But I'd like to think that when the sun is setting, when our differences have taken us all over the neighborhood, we can come home to each other. We can nestle in like brave little sisters and lean on each other for rest and sanctuary. We can tell our tales ("You'll never guess where I went today . . .") and hear about the paths we didn't take, but we'll know at the end of the day that we belong together.

I hope our community is marked by grace and affirmation instead of defensiveness and exclusivity. Sure, some wander down paths we don't understand, but there is room in the neighborhood for all of us. Ultimately, sisterhood is a soft place to land, and we can send each other out with full blessings knowing we can safely come home to one another. I want to be ever *for* you, and you for me.

Let's lay down our junk, our wonky junk that messes up relationships and community and togetherness. We won't let our own crazy stop us from affirming each other and banging the drum for our sisters. Our tribe does need not be ruled by scarcity; there is enough for every woman to live beautifully. A rising tide lifts every boat in the harbor; when one woman rises, we all rise. Let's open our hands and give it all away—esteem, honor, attention, love. What's good for one is good for all.

I see you, cheering each other on and calling forth the best in one another, and it slays me. This is the stuff. This is what we were made for. This is how to live well. If we prefer each other as Jesus told us to, there is nothing our community of women cannot handle. Give it to us: injustices, struggles, suffering, loss, heartbreaks, obstacles, *life*. We got this, together. Within this community, we strengthen each other to love our families and neighbors and cities and world. We point each other to God and call out our blessedness. It is so incredibly powerful.

I am so grateful to be a woman, here, with you, in our generation. Cup overflowing.

This is it. This is our one life. Let's go for it together.

I love you so.

Thank-You Notes For Real
(Acknowledgments)

I want to thank my friends because I would be bereft without you (and I would have no stories for this book). I am friend-rich and I know it, and I feel undone about it all the time. You make my life so happy. You are every funny, fun, kind, thoughtful, hilarious, smart, loyal, good thing in the universe. If you ever leave me, I will kill you in your sleep. (Sorry. That just got weird.)

So much love to my wonderful readers. You have been with me through countless books, studies, trips, the dentist, *Friday Night Lights* marathons, good times, hard times, all the times. Brandon always tells me, "Your people are so nice to you." YOU ARE. You are terribly special to me. I adore what we have. I cherish the space we've built together. I love you as much as Tim Riggins.

I cried through every essay about the church, because I love mine so. Church has been such a winding road for me, and in

Austin New Church, I'm just home. You are literally the best people I know. You love us and our city and world so well, I just can't believe it. Thank you for restoring to me what you didn't even know I had lost.

Thanks to my parents, Larry and Jana King, for being the best parents I never even knew to be grateful for when I was young. I thought all parents were affirming and loving and healthy and wonderful. I hope my kids feel about us one day the way I feel about you, namely, incredibly affectionate whilst living in their own homes and not my basement. You are so great, I'm not waiting until you are dead so I can write a memoir about your dysfunction like some of my friends. You're welcome.

To my agent, Curtis Yates, his incomparable wife Karen, colleague Mike Salisbury, and the whole Yates Dynasty, to quote Sealy: I am so grateful to be a horse in your stable. Curtis, you are agent, coach, male cheerleader, protector, and brother. And you've mastered emoticons and you know how I feel about that effort. Thanks for starting your own Supper Club after reading this manuscript. Thank you for crying tears of laughter when you read "Fashion Concerns." Thank you for believing in me and making me better and braver.

Enormous shout-out to my whole new Thomas Nelson team! Wow, you guys. Just wow. Brian Hampton, Chad Cannon, Emily Lineberger, Katy Boatman, Kristen Parrish, and the whole Nashville crew . . . I hardly know how to handle your big goals and big ideas and big confidence and big support. You've dreamed impossible dreams around my farmhouse table. You ate ox tongue sliders because I asked you to. *You let me speak in front of your entire company.* Be mine forever. I cannot find enough thank-you words.

Finally, thanks to my little family, the family of my dreams. You are everything I ever wanted. The Family Years are about to start changing, but I could not be more grateful (and DEVASTATED, but this section is supposed to be happy). Gavin, Sydney, Caleb, Ben, and Remy: you are my five favorite kids on planet Earth. I love and like you (and will absolutely stop paying your phone bill if you don't call me constantly from college next year, GAVIN. Twice a day should be sufficient). Brandon, look at our little life. Can you believe it? I know you can't because we constantly say, "Can you believe our life?" I don't know a husband who loves his wife and kids more. You are so for us and we know it. You make us all so happy. I love you. I really do. And I'm sorry about that time I threw all the Scrabble tiles on the floor.

I don't even know how to thank two groups of people:

My Launch Team and #the4500.

These women (and #bandoffour men) came together months before this book released, and a community emerged that I could not have imagined in my wildest dreams. What started with a simple rally around *For the Love* turned into meet-ups, scholarships, prayer groups, trips, parties, parenting threads, writing clubs, group merchandising, and essentially, the entire message of FTL demonstrated in real life. Friends, I love you with my entire heart. Beyond the beautiful endorsements and encouragement, you showed me that a FTL community is not only possible, it is vibrant and spiritual and unified and entirely irreverent. You are my best gift this year. Forever #onmybeam.

Thank you *For the Love* Launch Team members:

Abby Ades
Abby Twarek
Alaina Falk
Alia Joy Hagenbach
Alicia Vela
Aline Nahhas
Alison Stow
Allison Funke Pickett
Allison Ramsing
Aly Garrett
Alysa Bajenaru
Alyssa De Los Santos
Amanda Brown
Amanda Bush
Amanda Jo
Amanda Johnson
Amanda Kay Duckett
Amanda Pierce Jones
Amanda Rosler
Amanda Schafer
Amanda Smith Carver
Amanda Tomzak Regas
Amanda Wissmann
Amber Gonzales
Amber O'Toole
Amber Thompson Austin
Amberly Noble
Amilee Blanchard
  Sanders
Amity Rider Jones
Amy Cashion Hickman
Amy Crouch Wiebe
Amy Davis
Amy Dieter Decker
Amy Elizabeth Patton
Amy Mathias Austin
Amy Sheehan Wilkins
Anastasia Huffman

Andi Edwards
Andrea Grieshaber-
  Roberts
Andrea Stunz
Andrea Trexler Conway
Angela Brandel Gifford
Angela Gottschalk
Angie Abbate Mood
Angie Brown
Angie Dailey
Angie Kay Webb
Ann Crawford Goade
Ann Marie Corgill
Anna Carpenter
Anna Price
Anna Rendell
Anna Rubin
Annaliese Wink
Anne Henninghausen
  Alley
Anne Rumley Gift
Anne Watson
Annie White Carlson
AnnieLaurie Walters
April Golden
April Lakata
Ashlee Barlow
Ashley Abbott Bunnell
Ashley Behn
Ashley Besser
Ashley Doyle Pooser
Ashley Griffin
Ashley Pratt
Ashley Williams
Athena Buckner Davis
Aubrey Stout
Audra Ohm
Aundi Kustura Kolber

Becca Longseth Kiger
Becky Gillespie Yurisich
Becky Goerend
Becky Ritta
Becky Waldrup Johnston
Beth Buchanan Webb
Beth Latshaw-Foti
Beth Walker
Bethany Alexander
Bethany Beams
Bethany Winter Vaughn
Betsy Perrell Shaak
Brandee Holland
Brandi Dowdy
Brandi Ebersole
Brandy Lidbeck
Brenna Lauren
Brenna Stanaway
Briana DuPree
Brianna George
Brianna Sweet
Bridgette Cook
Brittany Roof Griffin
Brooke Justus Fradd
Bryna Richter Rodenhizer
Caitlin Snyder
Cara Joyner
Cara McConnell
Carey Schmitz Gregg
Carlee Ann Easton
Carol Fruge
Carrie Beth Tigges
Carrie Bricker Himel
Carroll Tatge Marxen
Cathy Campos Davidson
Celine Noyes
Chelsia Checkal
Cheryl Moses

Chris Bishop
Christian Annette
 Barnett
Christi Gibson Miller
Christine Frank Bowin
Christine Miller
 McDermott
Christy LeRoy
Christy Wiseman Leake
Cindy Battles
Claire Thompson
 Mummert
Colleen Crocker
Connie Martin Beckham
Corie Clark
Corie Gibbs
Courtney Banceu
Courtney Oakes
Courtney Smith Cassada
Courtney Thrash
Crissy McDowell
Crystal Santos
Cydney Reagan Feltcher
Cynthia M. Milner
Dana Pierce Herndon
Dana Rollins Martin
Danielle Brower
Darcie Tisdel Jackson
Darla Dillahunty Baerg
Dawn Klinge
Deanna Kell
Debi Jenkins
Deedra Amsden Mager
Deidre Price
Delia Jo Ramsey
Dena Howard Franco
Denise Kinsey Tyriver
Diana Kerr
Diane Weaver Karchner
Elise Cleary
Elise Johnson
Elizabeth Grossman
Elizabeth Lovell Lovelace
Elizabeth Sawczuk

Ellen Rorvik Frens
Embu Tshimanga
Emily Bedwell
Emily Carlton
Emily Davis Nelson
Emily Donehoo
Emily Judge Kates
Emily Mastrantonio
Emily McClenagan
Emily Tuttle
Emma Kathryn Robinson
Erica Armstrong
Erica Willer Groen
Erin Bassett
Erin Brazofsky
Erin Eichorn Shafer
Erin Felder Earnest
Erin Leigh Cox
Erin Moffitt
Erin Needham
Erin Vande Lune
Erin Wevers
Erin Woods
Gail Zainea Ramesh
Genevieve Yow
Geoff Kullman
Georgette Beck
Gina Grizzle
Ginger Newingham
Gloria S. Lee
Grace Manning
Gwendolyn Howes
Hailey Liew
Hannah Card
Hannah Lane Buchanan
Harmony Harkema
Heather Arseneault
Heather Galyon-Lamb
Heather Gerwing
Heather Goyne Parker
Heather Jasinski Brady
Heather Long
Heather Meek Henderson

Heather Middeldorf
 Rattray
Heather Post Hefter
Heather Webb
Heather Schmidt
Helen Kerr
Holly Kemp Garin
J'Layne Sundberg
Jack Donkin
Jack and Emily Engle
Jadee Isler
Jamie Brown
Jason Mitchell
Jeane Wynn
Jeanna Martin
Jemelene K. Wilson
Jen Gash
Jen Goforth
Jen Ruble
Jenna Sasso
Jenni DeWitt
Jennie Woelpern
Jenniemarie Palomo
 Cisneros
Jennifer Battles
Jennifer Davis
Jennifer Drennan Bell
Jennifer Hermosillo
Jennifer Howard
Jennifer Lloyd Goodwin
Jennifer Marcy Mrochek
Jennifer N. Early
Jennifer Snyder
Jennifer Wier
Jenny Garwood
Jenny Johnson Ross
Jenny Lyn Harwood
Jess Collier
Jessica Feeley
Jessica Hamlet
Jessica Hurtt
Jessica Laine Singletary
Jessica Morrison Grant
Jessica Turner

Jessica Wolfe
Jill Richardson
Jinny McCall
Jo Hooper
Joana Studer
Jodi Lynn McCoy
Jody Leigh
Johanna Trainer
Julie Moorhead
Julie Shreve
Julie Shumate Long
Kacy Wansley Pleasants
Kaitlyn Bouchillon
Kamryn Schill
Kande Koogle Milano
Kara McLendon
Kara Williams
Karen Taylor Graham
Karen Wolf Anderson
KariAnn Loy Lessner
Karli Von Herbulis
Kate Hight-Clark
Kate Scoggins
Katelyn Roskamp
Kathryn Giese
Kathy Macheras
Katie Corley
Katie Eller
Katie Howard
Katie Hurst
Katie May Tramonte
Katie McGee McReynolds
Katie Melton
Katie Mumper
Katie Vale
Katy Ruehr Epling
Katy Zitzmann
Kayla Aimee
Kayla Craig
Kelley Maranto Mathews
Kelly Buddenhagen
Kelly Buist
Kelley Dorgan Ruark
Kelly Ivey Johnson

Kelley Richards Smith
Kelsey Ferguson
Kelsey Holson
Kelsey King
Keri Snyder
Kiah Maylynn Geleynse
Kim Knudsvig
Kim Labar
Kimberly Bolden
Kimberly Hollis Widmer
Kimberly Poovey
Kirsten Trambley
Kodi BeVelle
Krista Gradias
Krista Wilbur
Kristen Bulgrien
Kristi Bair Roddey
Kristi James
Kristin Maddox Cheng
Kristin Stewart
Kristin Ulrikson-Hernke
Laine Alves
LaRae Humes
Laura Daniels
Laura Nile
Laura Zandstra Murray
Lauren Douglas
Lauren McHam Gibbins
Lauren McMinn
Leanne Johnston
LeeAnna Smith
Leslie Armstrong
Leslie David Carlton
Leslie Knight
Linda Shaffer Perkins
Lindsay Brandon-Smith
Lindsay Burden
Lindsay Langdon
Lindsay Prout Loughrin
Lindsay Stevenson
Lindsey Bryan
Lindsey Morgan Nihart
Lisa Bartelt
Lisa Ray Janes

Lisa Van Engen
Lisa-Jo Baker
Liv Campbell
Liz Wine
Lori Florida
Lori Harris
Lori Kuney Sawyer
Lori Stilger
Lori Waltmon Motal
Loyce Pickett
Lyndi Schnelle
Mabe Jackson
Macy Robison
Madelyn Jackson
Mandy Santos
Mandy White Alexander
Mariah Sanders
Marie Gregg
Marie Underhill Jackson
Megan Byrd
Megan Lowmaster
Melinda Hoggatt Mattson
Melinda Nelson
Melissa Crawford
Melissa Gardner-Miller
Melissa Henderickson
Melissa Jorgensen
Melissa Madole-Kopp
Melissa Neuman
Melody Consuela
   Taloolah Kopp
Meredith Donkin
Michele Lewandowski
   Mayhan
Michelle Collins
Michelle Craig Discavage
Michelle Fortik
Michelle Haseltine
Michelle Kelly
Michelle Kime
Michelle Robinson
Michelle Unwin
Miguel Cain Cooper
Mindy Christianson

Miranda Norris Coker
Miriam Blankenship
  Boone
Monica Jakoby Deskins
Monica Montoya
Natalie Bradley Slusser
Natalie Emmert Reid
Nichole Aponte Carrabbia
Nicole Case
Nicole Pals Diehl
Nicole Stormann
Noelle Morin
Pam Parker
Pamela Anne
Parker Barnes
Pattie Reitz
PenniCrouch Zylka Van
  Horn
Perri Verdino-Gates
Phillip and Shannon
  Taylor
Rachel Legg
Rachel Mueller Hill
Rachel Ravellette
Raleen Sloan
Rebecca Beckett
Rebecca Reardon Degeilh

Rebecca White Greebon
Rebekah Fairley
Rebekah Johnson
Robin Lee
Robin Parks Allen
Robin Turner Dauma
Robin Tutwiler
Robin White
Ronna-Renee Jackson
Rosanna Mullet
Sandy Kaduce
Sarah Denley Herrington
Sarah Herbert
Sarah Markowski
Sarah May
Sarah Schultz
Sarah Varland
Shanna Leigh
Shannon Bradley Taylor
Shannon Imel
Shawnna Householder
Shea Callahan Hughes
Sheila Burger Stover
Sheila Taylor
Shellie Carson
Shelly Mowinkel
Stacey Lynn Drake

Stacey Philpot
Stefanie Cullum Ritz
Stephanie Bishop
Stephanie Clinton
Stephanie English
  Roberts
Stephanie Kandray
Stephanie Lloyd
Stephanie Vos
Sue Bidstrup
Susan Galbo Hunt
Suzanne Sample Rees
Tamara Lancaster
Tammy Lee
Tara Davis
Tara Rooks
Terri Gorton Fullerton
Terry Dean Felix
Theresa Brown
Tomi Bussey Cheeks
Torrey Swan
Traci Adkins Cook
Tricia Klein
Valerie Cronk Kushnerov
Vicki Lodder
Whitney Cornelison
Whitney Severns Werling

Notes

Chapter 2: On Turning Forty

1. Maya Angelou, quoted in Maria Popova, "Maya Angelou on Identity and the Meaning of Life," *Brainpickings.org*, accessed January 4, 2015, http://www.brainpickings.org/2014/05/29 /maya-angelou-on-identity-and-the-meaning-of-life.
2. Annie Dillard, *The Writing Life* (New York: HarperPerennial, 1989), 32.

Chapter 3: On Calling and Haitian Moms

1. Anna Quindlen, *A Short Guide to a Happy Life* (New York: Random House, 2000), PDF e-book.

Chapter 6: Not Buying

1. Yes, Gwyneth Paltrow really did say this in a 2011 interview with *Elle* magazine. For more Gwyneth-isms, see: "10 Epic Quotes From Gwyneth Paltrow," *ABC News*, last modified March 26, 2014, http://abcnews .go.com/Entertainment/10-epic-quotes-gwyneth-paltrow /story?id=23070550.

Chapter 7: Tell the Truth

1. Brené Brown, *Daring Greatly: How the Courage to Be Vulnerable Transforms the Way We Live, Love, Parent, and Lead* (New York: Gotham Books, 2012), 248–9.
2. Scott Stratten, quoted in Brown, *Daring Greatly*, 171.
3. Brown, *Daring Greatly*, 99.

Chapter 12: Marriage: Have Fun and Stuff

1. Charlotte Brontë, *Jane Eyre* (New York: Carleton, 1864), 481.

Chapter 13: Jesus Kids

1. Drew Dyck, "The Leavers: Young Doubters Exit the Church," *Christianity Today* 54, no. 11 (November 1, 2010), 42.
2. Ibid., 40.
3. "Threads Presentation: What Matters to Young Adults?" SlideShare.net, posted by guest569c3f, January 8, 2009, http://www.slideshare.net/guest569c3f /threads-presentation-presentation.

Chapter 17: Quirky

1. Flo Rida and Will i Am, "In the Ayer," *Mail on Sunday*, Atlantic Records, 2008, compact disc.
2. Susan Cain, *Quiet: The Power of Introverts in a World That Can't Stop Talking* (New York: Crown Publishers, 2012), 230.
3. Ibid., 239.

Chapter 21: Poverty Tourism

1. Though the snapshot here is mine, it is inspired by the blog entry by Jamie Wright, "Healthy Short-term Missions? Do it like Jesus," *Jamie the Very Worst Missionary*, last modified April 10, 2012, http://www.theveryworstmissionary.com/2012/04 /healthy-short-term-missions-do-it-like.html.

Chapter 22: Dear Church . . .

1. Bo Lane, "Why Do So Many Pastors Leave the Ministry?" *ExPastors.com*, last modified January 27, 2014, http://www .expastors.com/why-do-so-many-pastors-leave-the-ministry-the-facts-will-shock-you/.
2. Ibid.
3. Bo Lane, "Why Do So Many Pastors Leave the Ministry?"; and Richard J. Krejcir, "Statistics on Pastors: What is Going on with the Pastors in America?" *IntoThyWord.org*, accessed January 4, 2015, http://www.intothyword.org/apps/articles/default .asp?articleid=36562.
4. Brown, *Daring Greatly*, 110.

Chapter 26: On Women

1. "Economic Empowerment," *HalftheSkyMovement.org*, accessed January 4, 2015, http://www.halftheskymovement.org/issues /economic-empowerment.

About the Author

Jen Hatmaker and her husband, Brandon, live in Austin, Texas, where they lead Austin New Church and raise their five kids (plus the chickens Jen said she would never own). She speaks at events all around the country and is the author of ten books, including *USA Today* bestseller *Interrupted* and *7: An Experimental Mutiny Against Excess*. Jen and Brandon starred in an HGTV series called *My Big Family Renovation* and live in a 105-year-old farmhouse with questionable plumbing.

Check out her ministry, schedule, and blog at
www.jenhatmaker.com.

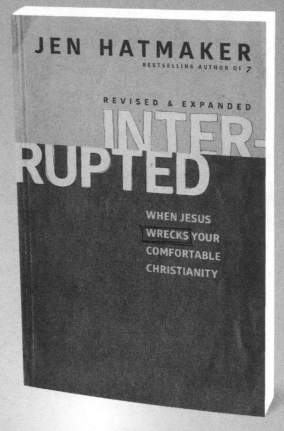